# A Year of Wonder

*Glimpses of God in Everyday Life*

C. David McKirachan

Westminster John Knox Press
LOUISVILLE • LONDON

*Book design by Sharon Adams*
*Cover design by Eric Walljasper, Minneapolis, MN*

*First edition*
Published by Westminster John Knox Press
Louisville, Kentucky

This book is printed on acid-free paper that meets the American National Standards Institute Z39.48 standard. ♾

PRINTED IN THE UNITED STATES OF AMERICA

03 04 05 06 07 08 09 10 11 12 — 10 9 8 7 6 5 4 3 2 1

**Library of Congress Cataloging-in-Publication Data**

McKirachan, C. David.
    A year of wonder / C. David McKirachan.—1st ed.
      p. cm.
    ISBN 0-664-22597-7 (alk. paper)
      1. Meditations. I. Title

  BV4832.3.M35 2003
  242'.2—dc21                                        2002023991

# Contents

# Beginning

Beginning

# Wandering

*I*t's snowing outside. But this snow doesn't match the pictures on the Christmas cards that arch over the doorways to the dining room. Every once in a while thunder growls and the wind pushes the monster dandruff around the corner of the house with a moan left over from Halloween. It's great.

Great it may be, but now that I've done all the laundry that needs doing and cleaned up the kitchen and watched Bob Vila install a kitchen, I realize I may not be going anywhere soon. Most of the world is in a similar fix. The airports are closed and the trains are bogged. Times Square may be rather sparse tomorrow on New Year's Eve. The tunnels into the City are probably plugged.

I score as a raving extrovert on those tests we take to find out who we really are and why we can't get along with other people. Extroverts crave human interaction. Add that to my twenty-first-century American obsession with doing and you can see why my nose is pressed against the window.

I enjoy meditation. I found it to be of value both times I tried it. (That was a little joke.) I know techniques for centering and calming the frantic and frazzled spirit. I teach them to folks and recommend them for their times of difficulty. But at times when I want to "find my center," or whatever it's called lately, I go on wanders through the world that surrounds me. I don't know if this is true meditation or contemplation or a function of an overactive imagination and an undisciplined mind. In any case, I write them down. It creates a map, a cartography of wonder.

I don't recommend my wanders to anyone as an exercise of philosophy or theology or any other systematic discipline. Neither do I see them as a meditative guide. So what good are they? They keep me out of trouble. They help me see the light that shines in the world. They punch holes in my arrogance. They take me beyond the detail and busy-ness that infests my reality. They're fun. All of that is what they are, for me. What they are for you may be another story altogether. Perhaps they can be a map for your wanderings.

The old year is grinding to a standstill, buried under the weight of a blizzard. So much has happened in a year. And when the storm clears, so much more will happen, right out into the new year. I need to find my big green rubber boots and go tromp around in the white stuff. Wanna come?

*Lord of Time, lead us out into your world,*
*That we might see*
*It,*
*Each other,*
*And You.*
*Amen.*

# January

# Zeros or Os

*I*t's the new year. Strange. As we count off these small numbers, 03, 04, 05, I get the feeling we're moving away from something. As if with the passing of the century, we left some other country behind. This new one feels a little shaky. Maybe the explosion of the millennium destabilized it all. I guess that's what traditions are for. They carry us over the *booms*.

I have a lot of traditions. Some of them are shared with the general population: Thanksgiving turkey and Christmas trees. Some of them are specific to the community here, like ringing the bell on Christmas Day and singing "Peace, Peace" along with "Silent Night" on Christmas Eve. There are those that were handed down to me by my family: We have to have a rutabaga on the table at Thanksgiving, even if no one eats it. Then there are those that are outgrowths of my own living, my own style of life: my collection of angels, and having the church over for coffee hour during Advent. It's fairly clear how most of these get started. But once in a while something is a bit of a gift.

I came home from the Thanksgiving extravaganza this year to find a box had fallen off the high shelf in my closet. It had been a ceramic Christmas decoration: the word *JOY*, with angels holding on to each letter. Expectably, the box made Rice Krispies sounds when I picked it up—so much for JOY. But I poked around to see what was left. One of the angels had broken loose and was intact, and the letter O, cushioned by the others, was undamaged. I put the angel on a high molding and the O on the windowsill in my bedroom. It is now my Christmas "O." A fitting and appropriate statement when considering the glory and wonder of Christmas. Also a new tradition.

This New Year will be filled with anxiety and perhaps even some broken plans. If we can approach these possibilities with something other than dread, there might be surprises waiting for us, even in the wreckage. How about if each of us looks for a new tradition for ourselves this year? Something that will build a bridge from here to there. Something to remind us that we've made it through again. Something to turn zeros into Os.

And who knows which of these will become something that future generations will revere us for. I really have to look into the commercial possibilities for mass-producing Christmas Os. What d'ya think?

*Lord of the possible, Lord of the known,*
*Open our known to your possibilities*
*Today.*
*Amen.*

# Epiphany

*I* was taking the ornaments off the Christmas tree today, packing them away. Did you ever notice that they never fit into the spaces they came out of? Next year they won't fit into the ones I put them into this year. I think it's a law of physics. Anyway, I was packing away when I noticed, across the room, my crèche.

The crèche in the McKirachan home is a dynamic affair. Evolving from windowsill to table, journeying toward the manger. The wise men are the last to arrive. They don't get there until January 6. That's Epiphany. They and their camels move from there to here in stages during Advent and the twelve days of Christmas, always coming closer to the star-crowned crowd of shepherds and sheep and Mary and Joseph and the babe and donkeys and cows and the attending mob of angels. The magi have a couple angels of their own, but they are more to bless than to guide. The wise guys have the star. My son Benjamin chose it when he was four. It's clear plastic. It matches the Limogue and antique German and Neapolitan angels, sort of. I wrapped gold ribbon around it and let it fall down, star fire and all that. So, the wise men have the star to follow.

What I noticed across the room was that the wise men hadn't made it to the manger. They and their camels and their angels of blessing were on the heater under the window about four feet—but a lot further if you take scale into account—from their goal. They had come a distance. They were on their way. But they hadn't made it yet, and it was January 7th. They were late for a rather important appointment. Oops.

I stopped packing and sat down, there by the crèche. I considered the journey these guys had taken. They'd come all the way from the end table over in the East. I wondered if they minded being late. I sat on the couch and wondered about their journey and mine. I wondered about being late.

And I decided. I decided it is more important to get there than it is to get there on time. And more important than getting there is getting on the road to begin with. I decided we worry too much about agendas and schedules, and not enough about how we're getting along and with whom we're getting along. And I decided it is more important to keep the star in sight than it is to know where it's leading.

So I moved the three of them to the manger; they deserved it. And I brought their camels and the blessing angels. And I decided the crèche would stay up a few more days to honor the arrival of the entourage from the heater by the windowsill in the East.

Now I have to take the lights off the tree.

*Lord of all journeys, may we remember*
*Who planned*
*The trip.*
*Amen.*

# Resolutions

*I* was talking to someone the other day about a habit I'd like to break. It was one of those conversations that are nice but carry no weight. We were chuckling together about our mutual humanity. And the person said, "Why don't you try making a New Year's resolution about it?" I responded with some polite pleasantry and we parted.

About ten minutes later that comment hit me like a rubber band that stretched out and snapped back. Thwapp! New Year's resolution. I could draw a line in time and use it to alter myself. What a weird idea. It might even work. What would I want to change? Then reality reasserted itself and reminded me of inertia and gravity and all the other things that make us sag. How could I change? I've been working on these bad habits for years. I've got them almost perfected. I just slip into them every time the opportunity presents itself. Change? That would mean thinking about how I act and what I say and what I do. That would mean trying and failing and trying again and sweat and guilt. I've gotten used to the twinges I get from the old bad habits. I know what to do with them when they come up. I'm used to looking in the mirror and seeing those warts. Remove them?

But the damage was done. That nice innocent comment had gotten under my skin. I knew the source of the discomfort. I had been nudged before by you-know-who. I was familiar with the feeling. I proceeded to complain to the source of my comfort and a lot of my creative discomfort, "Why can't you leave me alone? Every time I settle down, you get in the middle of things and move everything around. New Year's resolutions?" I protested cynically, "How juvenile! I'd think after all the eons you've had to work on technique you'd come up with something a bit more profound." Pretty weak, huh? I'd swear I could hear a chuckle. I must be a huge source of humor for the Almighty.

So now I've been thinking. What do I want to focus on changing? Lots of fun. I've got to make a list. That way it's harder to cheat. Hmmm. Maybe this won't be too bad.

But there's no way I'm giving up coffee.

*Lord of all change, may I be open*
*To your potential*
*In my life.*
*Amen.*

# Jetties

*I* walked alone up to the end of the dark road, through the fences and over the dunes to the beach. There were few lights along the street and none on the beach. Only the distant reflected glow of some distant store lit the chilly, lonely night.

The winter sea broke over the jetties. I could only see them dark and immobile when the black water foamed to white as the swells found these stolid defenders standing between the deep sweep of the sea and the land. These were massive stones, cut and brought from who knows where and piled here to protect the fragile beach and dunes from the tides and storms that would beat and tear at our island.

There on that lonely beach our arrogance amazed and embarrassed me. For how long has the sea swept the land and moved these frail sandbars and dunes, creating ever-changing patterns of barrier and inlet? And we in our desire to protect our structures of wood and glass drop these stones in the ocean's way, as if they could alter the power of the sea and its child, storm. As I stood in the cutting wind I realized how small even our best efforts are in the face of that heaving darkness that could and has carried away the most massive jetty in a single night. And I felt so small, there in the darkness, standing at the edge of another deeper darkness pounding at the very land beneath my feet. Every best effort seems worth so little when the storms blow.

We work so hard to build and protect our structures. They are precious to us. And because of our investment we delude ourselves about their durability and permanence. All the time, they are constructions whose very foundations are laid on the shifting terrain of now's frail stability. And so close and oh so powerful is the tide that carries all into darkness.

I stood alone, in awe of our arrogance and our vulnerability, chilled by much more than the winter wind blowing out of the northeast. A storm on its way. And I shivered in the wind. Can despair be far from anyone who sees and understands how temporary and ephemeral we are?

Mostly to defend my small soul from power too great to carry or contest, I turned my back on the dark expanse, and there, like a small star in the night, burned the light above the door of my house. And I remembered something more eternal than all the structures or defenses and more powerful than all the waves pushed by the winds of storm. And I walked down from the darkness, back toward the light and warmth of home.

*Lord of the storm and darkness, may I not fear*
*My own fragility.*
*Or you.*
*Amen.*

# February

# Tingle and Glow

*T*his is a dark month. January shines with the reflected glory of Christmas. February is one more step away from warmth and light, and there's still a distance to go till spring. It's a month when we have to plan vacations just to keep from getting down in the dumps. Ash Wednesday usually happens in February. Now there's a real giggle.

The calendar planners knew this. They sat in their tower (all mystically wise people sit in towers) and leaned over the charts and manuscripts, grumbling, "We've got a dark one here. What shall we do?" The lumpy one, who had to stand on his chair to lean over the charts and manuscripts, pushed his tall and pointed hat back (it tended to fall down to his nose) and squeaked (he was short in the resonance department too), "Let's have a party." The others turned to him and glowered (they tended to look down on him in more ways than one). "Let's put one on the calendar," he rushed on, "a celebration. Not a big one, but just big enough to make 'em tingle and glow."

So, it is on the fourteenth that the darkness is lit by a tingle and glow. Yeah, I know, Hallmark, florists, and Godiva set the whole thing up (I like the story about the guys in the tower better). But on the other hand there is the tingle and glow. There is the tingle of getting those pop-out pictures in the second grade that say "Be Mine." And the little candy hearts that taste terrible with the cute sayings on them. And the glow of the lace-and-glue creations that come out of lumpy envelopes. And oversized envelopes filled with a heady stew of sentiment and passion all stirred together. And flowers.

Have you heard they've isolated the enzyme of love? So when I get all flustered and soupy about my honey, it's blood chemistry. Not real romantic, is it? But even if that's how it works, what better time to celebrate the enzyme of passion than amid the slush and flu? And if it is an enzyme—a chemical released and disbursed within us for the purpose of drawing us together over the distances of self-protection and preservation—then let us celebrate the enzyme and the pump that disburses it. Let us laud this chemical released in us that lets us giggle at homegrown poetry and drip and sniff at gestures from the pump (that's the heart).

So, whether you believe in wizards in a tower or corporate plots or enzymes, I hope you get some Valentines (that almost rhymes). They're good for you. And I hope you send some. They're good for everybody. And don't forget the short lumpy guy with the big hat. After all, it was his idea to begin with.

*Lord of pumps and enzymes,*
*Roses are red, violets are blue.*
*You made me to love,*
*I thank you.*
*Won't you be my Valentine?*
*Amen.*

# Vicissitudes of a Weatherman

*P*unxsutawney Phil lives in a large glass box in a public library. He's well fed and fat and probably very content for most of the year. Food shows up on time, and his accommodations get cleaned regularly. He has places to hide from the inquiring glances of humans using the library, some of who come there just to see him. And since they put in a Mrs. Phil, life has been peachy, just fine and dandy. That is, until that day when he is dragged out of his comfortable home and brought outside into the cold February air. He is then put into another box, one that is not glass. Seen from the outside it resembles a tree stump. Then Phil is grasped by the nape of his neck and pulled out into the early morning light to the concerted cheers of ten to fifteen thousand onlookers, who grow quiet only long enough to hear a proclamation boomed from loud speakers. Phil's fame lasts only a few minutes and is probably terribly uncomfortable and utterly confusing for him. But such is the fate of groundhog weathermen.

I don't know what the proclamation said this year. If it was good news or bad, Phil doesn't care. He's back home in the library.

There is a Chinese curse: "May you be granted an interesting life." Periodically I come to understand that curse when my priorities and my resources make war. There are so many pulls and pushes that fray our lives. They take away our comfort and confuse us. And half the time we get blamed for things we didn't even try to do. Then we fervently wish for the safety of our boxes.

But if we are to be anything, if we are to become more than "existers," to add something to the world, perhaps we must be willing to expect the discomfort of "coming out of our boxes" to accept our role in the confusing drama of life as it unfolds. Perhaps we'll get blamed for something, perhaps we'll be cheered, most likely both. But wouldn't it be sad to never have had any of the discomfort so wonderfully available in an interesting life?

I hope Phil has a sense of humor. It blunts the critics.

*Lord of miracles and normality,*
*May we remember*
*There is more to life*
*Than our boxes.*
*Amen.*

# Setting Out

*T*he painting was of a sailboat, a good-sized sloop with a bowsprit, mainsail, and Genoa jib, full of tropical wind under a sky that could redefine blue. About thirty-five feet, setting out, heeled over on a broad reach from a palm-shadowed cove to some other clear water anchorage that would cradle the crew in an evening swim before they had a cold drink and a sunset-tinted dinner. It was a dream of color and concept, and it hung outside a room on the cancer ward, a room full of pain and the diminishing circles of life that bring us all down to grieving.

Each time I came down that hall I did what I always do when facing the beasts of fear and pain and confusion. I inhaled and tried to be part of the Life of the world. But I was tired. Spirit and body and mind were a bit bruised as I sat vigil. I had a sense of loss, as if the gift of life had become a memory that shone on another day when Santa Claus was real and I had fewer disappointments to remember. What difference did my presence make as we faced these dark powers? So I looked out into the hall, and there it was.

I wondered at it. It was as if the breeze that filled those sails gained access to my mind, that bright sun warmed my hands, so powerless in this battle. The painting did not take me away; it brought me back, back from that place of indefinite shadows and weak words. It offered me a view of value and glory that surged beyond any room or harbor out into the deeps where the gulls are fellow travelers and their cries punctuate the wind's crack and the wake's low roar.

It reminded me that in this moment of life there rests a gift that cannot be denied, no matter what the weight or cramp that must be borne. It does not shine on some other place where everything is open to the sun. It shines here, here in each spirit that can see through dim limitations out to where we are going, out into possibility.

> Sunset and evening star,
>     And one clear call for me!
> And may there be no moaning of the bar,
>     When I put out to sea.*

I wonder if they knew what they were doing when they hung that painting on that wall. I wonder.

> *Father of the far reaches,*
> *Mother of the deep,*
> *My sails are frail,*
> *My skill is weak.*
>
> *My craft an offering.*
>
> *Take us out, along Dawn's dancing path*
> *With hope's glory calling,*
> *And may we find at sunset's bell*
> *Home's warm embrace waiting.*
>
> *Receive us on our way.*
> *Amen.*

---

* Alfred Lord Tennyson, "Crossing the Bar," from *Demeter and Other Poems* (London: MacMillan, 1889).

# One of Those Days

*I* walked into my office the other day with the usual pivot and swirl. The door escaped control and banged into the work-table. A pile of papers overbalanced and hit the floor. I dropped my briefcase at just the right angle to prop it against my desk. It bumped a partially opened drawer and fell over. My calendar escaped from the case and slid under my chair. I dropped my keys. They slid off the desk and joined the papers and my calendar. I peeled off my jacket. It was glad to get rid of me. The hangers had arranged themselves in a tangle during the night. Did you know they giggle just before you open the door? It's a setup. Three of them fell laughing when I lifted one. As I turned to deal with the rest of the day, I stopped.

At the edge of the paper swamp of my desk was a vase of glory. Lavender and purple miracles. I did not put them there. I did not ask for them. I could only stand and wonder at them. Which I did. They stopped me. They halted my pell-mell rush toward nowhere in particular and let me see again.

So often it is the small thoughts, the fragile gifts that exert this power. It is the kind, unasked-for touches that allow the rush and grind to be significant. This is how I understand grace, beauty that flows. It enters our lives and offers meaning. Often we are too preoccupied with speed and agenda, with fatigue and anxiety, to allow grace to exert its tender power. So, we live in pain, our clumsy efforts banging into life rather than appreciating its unexpected moments of glory.

They will wilt. Cut flowers do. But as I sit here considering, I realize that they have lived already beyond their petals and stems. They have become a gift. Perhaps that's what eternity is all about.

*God of grace and glory, thank you.*
*May I be open to receive*
*Eternity*
*Today.*
*Amen.*

# March

# Of Snowstorms and Tubas

*I*t's March. In like a lion, out like a lamb. This year the lion's kind of tame. The daffodils were coming up in February. But, every time I mention how spring is already here, someone is quick to remind me that winter is not gone and snow is a common occurrence at this time of year. "We could still have a whopper."

Sometimes I wonder why we are so prone to put the brakes on hope. We call it all kinds of things: being realistic, not denying the truth, keeping our feet on the ground. But whatever we call it, it points out the cloud in the sky, the crack in the wall, the bump in the plaster, the flaw in the dream. It quells excitement. It defends the holy "probably."

Statistical probability is interesting. There is an exception to every rule, including that one. That's why we have to say "probably" rather than "always." Do you know how many "probablies" have never happened? How about all the "probably nots" that did? Well, that still won't keep a March snowstorm off the driveway.

I don't know about that. If we are willing to really focus, *no snow, no snow, warm, warm, warm, warm,* why shouldn't it make a difference? If something as invisible as barometric pressure can give me a sinus headache, why can't I make it go back the other way?

At the very least there is no reason to cloud the skies of some dreamer whose garden is already blooming, within. Perhaps all of us can't be dreamers, and surely there is plenty of room for practicality, but isn't a smile worth cultivating? And if we pause, even in the chilly growl of March, to feel the gentle breath of what may be but isn't yet, doesn't it light the day a bit brighter to see in our mind's eye the garden that may be?

So watch out, all you practical folk. I'm becoming a militant optimist. Next time somebody reminds me of some "probably" that ought to be taken into account by any sane realist, I may parade right through their March snowstorm. Here come the tubas!

> *Lord of hope, may we be infected*
> *By life*
> *That in the midst of death*
> *We might live*
> *Abundantly.*
> *Amen.*

# The Great Communicator

*N*orma Jean is a familiar sight around the church. Since my "dumb" dog learned to open the backyard gate, she has become a fixture at any meeting that serves food. But if truth be told, she just likes people. She schmoozes with the best of them. Her way of saying hello and shaking hands may be a little rude by human standards, but that's how dogs check each other out.

Most of the time I look at animals with a rather paternalistic attitude. They are beautiful and have a right to life and *yada yada yada*. But underneath all my appreciation is a lack of acceptance of them as important spirits in my world. Norma blows that apart on a regular basis. She lets me know that though she may have the title "pet," she is not to be taken lightly.

If I look honestly at my relationships, it is not only dogs, cats, and otters—let alone lizards, vultures and gnats—that I consider apart like this. It is others of my own species. Sometimes it's even people I know and work with. I put them aside into a limbo of objectification. They walk and talk and I nod and smile, I even note the shape and symmetry of their features and their lives, but they are separate, other, apart from what is the core and center of my sense of identity. It is easy to watch from such a distance, watch and understand, even sympathize while not really taking them seriously. And if we leave them over there, we can judge and ignore them so much more easily.

The other day Norma got sick. I think she raided the garbage and paid for her binge. She made a number of messes in places we couldn't ignore and walked more slowly, wagged less, barked not at all. When I let her out she didn't even try to open the gate. I got worried. And again she was anything but "other." Her well-being, her pain and mortality touched and affected the size and shape of my life.

Perhaps we cannot embrace everything—our arms are not big enough, our souls do not have the floor space to keep all reality within. But the menagerie that lives in that territory has access to the size and shape of our lives and helps to determine who and what we are and what is important to us. Keeping that territory small may be more efficient and less risky, not to mention less messy, but it also reduces our world.

I'm glad Norma's nose is cold and wet again. I know some in the world consider her a pest and would rather that she kept her place. But I will try to love them anyway. And I won't worry too much when she says hello with that wet nose. Maybe she'll get through to them. She's a great communicator.

*Lord of us all, great and small,*
*Open us to your presence*
*In the least of these*
*And the great,*
*That we might welcome you*
*With tails and voices*
*Wagged and raised.*
*Amen.*

# Inertia

*I*t's about halfway through Lent and I'm ready for Easter. This six-week business is a couple weeks too long. I'm tired of the serious nature of the preaching series, and Lenten study on sacrifice, and the class on the long-suffering Job, and the focus on all the self-searching and mirror looking and repentance trying. Besides, we just lost an hour of sleep and I haven't even had time to put the fertilizer on my garden.

I remember when I used to run, and now when I ride my bike there are two humps I have to get over. The first is getting started. I have all kinds of excuses for preventing my getting going. Breaking that inertia of a body at rest takes some willpower. I deal with that by having clothes I wear to exercise. I put them on while I continue to make excuses. By the time I tie my sneakers, it's stupid to not get out and sweat.

The second hump is about ten minutes into the ordeal. It feels like I've punished myself enough. It doesn't make sense to waste any more time at this. Besides, by the time I get home it will be fifteen minutes that I've been challenging myself. Isn't that enough? And so the excuses run. No argument. They're all true. I don't fight. I just keep going.

And invariably, the second part of my sweat-fest is much more pleasant and easy and fun. And physically, that's when I get my best work done, now that I've warmed up and blown out the cobwebs.

There are usually humps in life, humps that prevent us from starting things and humps that stop us halfway down the road. They are real. And most of the time, there are very good reasons not to begin or keep going. But most of the time, if we are willing to find ways to keep moving, the other side of the hump is where many meaningful things happen.

So, I guess I won't quit Lent, even though I have all kinds of good excuses. Maybe I just need to get over this hump. After all, Jesus didn't quit, and boy, did he have a bunch of great excuses.

*Lord of the climbing way, I need an escalator.*
*May I begin,*
*May I follow,*
*May I turn again when I wander.*
*Lead me, Lord.*
*Amen.*

# John Wayne of Spring

*I*t was a surprise, on the verge of breaking into yellow bloom down behind the gas grills. It was either a leftover from some former garden or a volunteer, migrated to this hidden corner courtesy of an agent other than myself. The shelter of the surrounding equipment had held warmth that was bringing it to early flower despite lingering winter.

I stood there appreciating it, likening its placement and its arrogant denial of all the reasons that it should not be ready to bloom into its daffodil identity. Somehow it was more significant than all the beds and planned banks of cousins that were sprouting elsewhere. It stood alone and defiant and independent, a regular John Wayne of spring's troopers. But it was also vulnerable, alone, out of season, and out of the safety of places where flowers are expected.

Easter blooms. It comes as a celebration of global shift that will bring all the beds and banks of glory along. It affirms the growth and hope of spring. But in a deeper sense it is more than a celebration of the return of that which we hope for. Easter is a surprise. It blooms beyond our expectations and logic. It is out of place, exploding in the graveyard of normality and creating victory where tragedy has claimed the stage.

When we fit our celebration of Easter into the global

normalities of our lives, no matter how pleasant or hopeful they may be, we forget the insanity of the original. It did not fit the lives of those who were there. Their response was terror and disbelief. However, it was a fact. Out of place and out of logic, simply too nuts to be believed or understood. As such, this solitary soldier of a daffodil has much more in common with the empty tomb than some carefully tended garden. Its glory is unique and original, surprising and unsettling. And it is a precursor to that which is to come, a global shift from death to life to which it bears joyful evidence. For we shall all bloom, even as He did. Whatever the temperature of the garden or the tomb, spring and new life are coming into the world.

Allelujah.

*Lord of the surprise of Life, may we dare*
*To bloom*
*With Him*
*Whatever the season.*
*Amen.*

# April

# The Song of Life

He was so busy, so pulled and demanded.
He was so important, so followed and needed.
He was so feared, so watched and blamed.
He was so powerful, so focused and clear.

He was a man, walking on dusty roads.
He could only reach so far with
Hand and voice. He was a man.
He wanted that which could not be.

He tried, he reached, he cried, he slept.
He worked, he sweated, he ate, he smiled.
He wondered, he listened, he saw, he knew.
He wished, he touched, he felt, he prayed.

He had a family, of blood and of spirit.
He had friends, of arguments and fishing.
He had enemies, of fear and manipulation.
He had dreams, of hope like his for all.

I wonder what he did when his feet hurt and
His hands were sore from being grasped.
I wonder if he sang when he walked
On roads that took him far from home and rest.

I wonder, in the dark of that morning;
I wonder, did it all seem small, his life, his days,
Or did it rise up with him, each moment
Another cause for angels' song.


*Lord of resurrection, may my moments*
*Rise*
*With Him*
*To glory.*
*Amen.*

# Noodles and Prunes

*G*ood Friday has always bothered me. It bothered me when I was a kid. We "celebrated" the moment with a "feast" of noodles and prunes with croutons. I thought there was more sacrifice in this feast than in a total fast. I advocated for that in my teenaged years and was told to clean up my plate.

The older I got, the more it got under my skin. There were silences in the day. And when business went on as usual, it felt like it shouldn't. I finally got focused enough to consider *him* at the center of this whole thing and I found more uneasiness. It didn't seem to me that most of the people doing the talking about *him* were really dealing with what went on. They generally went one of two directions. The most common was the victim route.

He didn't seem like a very good victim to me. He was too intentional. He went into this with his head up. Where was the tragedy? It was ugly and nasty and painful, but it seemed to me, he knew where his actions and words were taking him, all the way down the line. And he didn't stand up for any grand cause. There is every evidence he just joined the parade of the recipients of Roman justice. So I never could buy the victim route.

The other popular position has always been the hero route. I liked this one more. I guess it appealed to my macho side.

See? He died like a man. But even that didn't wash real well. He seemed too sad to be macho. And without the flags and the causes to stand for, what kind of a hero could he be?

So if he wasn't a victim and he wasn't a hero, what was he?

What was left has disturbed me more than I'd ever been before I tried to figure it all out. And it continues to make me uneasy.

I've come to the conclusion that the cross is not a mistake or a battle or a tragedy. It's a normality. Anytime anyone dares to love unselfishly, a cross is there somewhere. It may not be made of blood-soaked timbers, and it may not kill someone in an afternoon, but depend on it, a cross will be there. All that happened to him was a function of his good love. That's what happens. He just made it real clear.

I may be wrong. I have been once or twice. And in some ways I hope I am about this. Because it means there's a cross out there for me. All I have to do is make the right choices and it's mine.

*Lord of living, lord of life,*
*If there is a cross for me*
*Today*
*May I remember him*
*And lift.*
*Amen.*

# The First Day of Summer on Mars

*E*aster is kind of a third-rate holiday. It barely causes a bump along the road of spring. Our churches do their best to get focused on it, with the introspection of Lent and the hoo-ha of Palm Sunday and the tension of Holy Week. But try as they might, Easter stays at the same level as the other holidays that rest below the peak season of Thanksgiving/Christmas/New Year's and the second-string days of Halloween, Labor Day, Memorial Day, and the Fourth of July. Easter sits there, without fireworks or trips to the beach or barbecues. Some folks have traditional meals, egg hunts, baskets full of goodies that show up out of nowhere, but all in all it's not that big a deal.

It makes a weird kind of sense. At the core of it is something that blows the whole order of things all askew. Resurrection. It makes a good basis for religious celebration, but what practical use is it? How do you sell it to people who have never seen life beyond life and who have all kinds of evidence of simple ordinary death on a regular basis? We may as well make a big deal about the first day of summer on Mars. It happens, but what impact does it have on us? He rose. OK. And this does what in my normality? Eternal life? Where and when? Someplace we can't see, and some when we're kind of unsure of. You begin to see why we stick to rabbits and eggs.

The first Easter was kind of a dud too. There were no choirs of angels to herd shepherds or stars to pull wise men. There were no official reactions or news interviews. There was only a bunch of freaked-out refugees, so scared they couldn't agree what to do. So they locked themselves in an upper room and bit their nails. They didn't know how to handle it either. Finally they went fishing.

But I think it all fits somehow. He was only one person. He was torn down and thrown away, a bad joke. He was a victim, but not a very grand one. There were no causes stood for, there were no flags waving, there were no huge injustices when he died. It was another day as usual, filled with the waste and brutality that most people did and do their best to avoid, but cannot deny, no matter how hard they try. He stood there caught in the headlights of the semi of status quo, and it squashed him flat. We've seen that happen before, to greater or lesser degrees. His rising didn't stop the eighteen-wheeler of normality. It still goes on.

But again it fits. Despite our attempts to glorify and segregate this whole thing from our living, it remains very humanly personal. The only difference this made or will ever make rests in whether we care about this one guy, or any one guy. If he's important to us as a person, not as an icon, then the whole thing matters. But if we try to pump this into some kind of abstraction or cause, there is only a blip on the interest scale.

If I was told somebody had risen from the dead, it wouldn't rock my world. It would be weird and distant. But if I was told my brother, whom I saw dead, was walking through walls and sitting down with some of his cronies for brunch, I'd set off running. And I would never see death or life in the same way again.

So I guess Easter, for all its fanfare, is intensely personal. And if you get to know this guy, it may remain rather low-key as a holiday, but everything else changes. Maybe Easter isn't about a holiday. Maybe it's about life.

*Lord of Life, may we care*
*Enough*

*To run*
*To the tomb.*
*Amen.*

# Heaven

*I* remember many things about my mother. To say that she was important to me is to be silly. She formed my life for years. She molded me. Her words of encouragement and hope, her view of the way things work, or ought to, her vision of beauty that saw the bloom in every patch of weeds and the potential of warmth and glory in each situation. My cousin said to me she was the youngest person he ever met.

I could say I remember her but it is different than that. She and my father and my brother are more than memories. They live in another place. The power of their lives cannot be denied by something as small as the lack of breath or heartbeat.

Before they died, I had little truck with heaven. I didn't worry about it. I found all sorts of support in Scripture and wisdom to carpe diem. And while I was seizing the day I remembered what the Lord said about the reign of God being much more in the here and now than in some future never-never land. Frankly, I had a hard time believing in something so pat as pearly gates and "harpathons." I spoke words of comfort to people in their grief, but it was as if the words never came back to me. There was no resonance in them for me. People I tried to help spoke with appreciation, spoke of the healing God offered them in their grief, and I was glad to be a part of it. It was a treatment I had never needed.

It is different now. It is as if there is a part of my world that I have never seen or been to but that is important to me because people I know and love live there. I speak the words of resurrection and hope now, and there is a power and resonance in them as clear as a shout that answers me back across the boundary of death. And though death is much more real to me, though it has content and shape it never had, I fear it less. For they have gone there before me, they whom I trust and know.

I look forward to meeting my Master, face to face, of listening and speaking and being with the one who has loved me throughout eternity. But I'll tell you a secret. I don't think I'll get to him for a while. I'll be busy. My family has never been known for being shy. I doubt whether heaven will have changed them much. And I have never known anything to come between my mother and her children. I don't think the Lord will mind. After all, we have eternity.

*Lord of eternity, may I live*
*Within touch and sight*
*Of your kingdom*
*Here.*
*Amen.*

# Giggles and Ahhs

*I* was walking down the sidewalk between Steamboat Springs and the wave pool at Blizzard Beach when I noticed the sprinklers were turned the wrong way. They were the low ones that send out a broad mist. These were spraying onto the sidewalk rather than into the flowerbeds. It felt great, so I stopped and splashed around on the wet pavement.

Florida sunshine tends to heat concrete until it feels like a frying pan. Let's say it's uncomfortable to feet and other body parts. The spray altered a painful tiptoe to a delightful interlude. I stopped splashing and stood there amazed. The sprinklers weren't turned the wrong way at all.

We went to Disney. That sentence in itself is a monument to understatement. Nobody can just *go* to Disney. It is a life experience. There is no other word to call the place than "World." It is an ecology that demands changes in how and what we see and feel and consider important. This seemingly impossible task is accomplished by sprinklers for hot feet and countless other details that take into account the frailty of the human beings that enter Mickey's world. Without any fanfare or announcement, the providing of simple human comfort and childish delight becomes the rule.

The discipline involved in this is boggling. It is an operation that is not only huge but is orchestrated and coordinated and maintained to a degree that is beyond imagination. From the minute to the gargantuan there is a consistency that encourages giggles and ahhs with every step. And all the design, engineering, and discipline centers around the purpose of treating people as if they were valuable. It made me consider some of the sharp edges I could remove in my life to make it a more giggle- and ahh-oriented place.

One night Mickey came and sat down at our dinner table. We communicated—he silently, we with a lot of laughter. We kidded around until he got up to leave. I stood up and shook his hand. I wanted to thank him. I wanted to somehow let him know it all worked. So there I stood, a grown man shaking a six-foot mouse's hand with tears in my eyes. "Thanks for the sprinklers, Mickey. You do good work."

What do you expect? He's a movie star.

*Lord of giggles and ahhs, forgive my arrogance.*
*A child let me be*
*That I might stand*
*Amazed.*
*Amen.*

# May

# Clearing Trend

We were coming home from a Florida vacation. It was warm and sunny in Florida, the way it's supposed to be when you go on vacation. My father-in-law picked us up at the airport. He asked how the weather had been. It was the normal, polite thing to do. But when I said it had been beautiful and asked him how it had been here, he proceeded to tell us about the Jersey flood. That was a Saturday. It had been raining for days by that point. Not drizzling or dripping, but raining, and raining, and raining. Drizzling and dripping were considered clearing trends. By the next Wednesday I stood outside and got wet in one of those clearing trends. At least I could look up and not see a ceiling.

I heard a weather report this morning. The announcer became fervent when he got to tomorrow. He spoke about the possibility of a sunny day. Something was different than the modulated tones usually spread like so much makeup across the weather map. There was something approaching authentic emotion coming through. He spoke about the sun like it was a visiting dignitary, the pope or the young princes from England. I found myself having a sensory memory. Warmth. My hands and feet, grown used to damp and chill, were remembering. Warmth, sunny warmth. I felt like Annie, singing "Tomorrow, it's only a day away."

Then I had a horrible thought. What if the weather dude was wrong, as weatherfolk so often are. What if all that predictive power packed into Doppler 4000 missed something. What if, instead of waking up to the visiting dignitary shining in the sky, we woke up to another day of—I don't want to say it—rain. How long could we go on? Would forty days do us in?

This was not a question of the capacity of our sump pumps. It was not even a question of flooding from swollen streams and lakes. It was a question of our spirits. It was a problem of limits and freedom, of entrapment and gray skies that put a lid on everything we see and know. There was no view, no way to reach beyond the grim surrounding dampness that was filling up every dip and hollow and breeding mildew far beyond our shower. Can you mow mushrooms? I felt like a character in an Alfred Hitchcock movie:

"Good evening. Tonight we will witness a man screaming in the rain." Growing more wild-eyed by the minute, I considered the constant thundering beast . . . RAIN! AAAR-RRGGGHHH!!!! (I get a little dramatic sometimes.)

I woke up this morning and the ruler of the sky was back in charge. There were some clouds, but they were proper, white fluffy things. My eyes stopped bulging and the blood pressure dropped. We'll be pumping for a while, until the water table drops below the dining room. Soggy will be the rule for a time, but the prison bars are gone. Now the days can bloom and May is back in charge. I vowed to appreciate the bits of blue and the reflections and shadows that are gifts so often left unappreciated. I also vowed, after a few moments of soaking up the light, not to reject the gift of the rain, when it comes again. But I hope I don't have to appreciate the wet gift for a while. I do a lot better when my shoes don't squish.

*Lord of freedom, may I learn to dance*
*In puddles*
*As gracefully*
*As in the sun.*
*Amen.*

# Cold Metal Bleachers

*W*e were at a Little League game the other night, a normal occurrence in this month of May. What was not so normal was the bone-chilling cold that made us get up and dance from one foot to the other, hands in pockets, necks scrunched into the spring jackets we'd worn. Until we were sitting in bleachers, we hadn't paid attention to the temperature.

What the heck is going on? This is May. Where are the sunshine and bees and iris and dreamy days that make it hard to keep track of whatever it was I was supposed to keep track of? Why am I doing a dance that belongs to late October? There are no red and orange trees. There are no pumpkins. That is baseball being played, not football. Why am I waltzing to keep warm?

I mentioned this to someone the next day, and the reply was, "Yep, typical Jersey spring." But wait a minute. Where have I been all these years, deluding myself about May? You mean it's never been soft and balmy? I just imagined all that?

I get the same feeling when I read about the "normal" state of affairs with the human race. Kids, parents, marriage, the church, and my local library have already gone down the tubes, according to the statistics and the experts who gather them. We are in the midst of deep darkness. So I guess when I enjoy kids, parents, marriage, the church, and my local library, I'm just being a lightweight and deny-ing the truth.

Delusional I may be, but it seems to me that the present tense, though full of difficulties, is not the horror it's cracked up to be. Though we have much negativity to face, we are not consigned to it as if it's some terrible curse that we must ignore or medicate away to celebrate the now.

Dancing there on the sidelines, I was and am absolutely certain of two things. One: There will be games played in balmy breezes. Spring is here and will comfort our chilled bones, soon. I insist on it. Two: Whatever the weather, I'm going to have a good time.

"No batta. No batta. Put it in there, pitcha." Let's do a "wave." It'll keep us warm.

*Lord of all blessing, may I accept*
*The time and place*
*Of your giving*
*That I may see*
*Your new day*
*Coming.*
*Amen.*

# Gravity

*I* have worn a size 12 shoe since my last growth spurt during college. I try shoes on but it is a ritual, as much to look at them on my feet as to consider their fit. What's to consider? I wear a 12. So when my running shoes were a bit snug, I thought it was something to do with the weather or something I'd catcn. But it didn't pass. So I thcn assumcd thc shocmakcr had made a mistake. They'd mislabeled an 11.

OK, so I'm slow.

I managed to live in denial very successfully until I began to consider buying a new pair. It's the Scottish blood. Cheap runs in it like some latent virus. I have outbreaks, like a rash, at the weirdest times. I couldn't consider replacing shoes that still had mileage in them. But I soon accepted the inevitable: My feet had spread to a larger size.

I've been watching myself age for quite a few years now. Hair graying and sprouting in unlikely places, reading at arm's length, glasses . . . but expanding feet? When I'd been growing I had a weird sort of pride about such change. But now it isn't growth; it's a response to the brutal forces of gravity. My feet are getting smooshed by my age. Nobody ever told me about this one. People giggle about glasses, they talk about hair, but feet? It's like some sort of betrayal. Feet are dependable. They're one of the givens in life. If they change, what's next? Is my nose going to droop?

I can see that I'm not going to be very graceful about this whole thing. I'll tolerate changes that I consider fair, within the rules, but don't surprise me with this weird stuff. "To every thing there is a season" better only apply to the "things" that I'm ready for.

But then again, it is sort of interesting looking for a new shoe size. It raises a whole new set of issues when I go hunting for footwear, different places in the store, different options. Salespeople to chase around for size 13s that may be in the back but don't fit on the display racks. And why shouldn't I be proud of my feet growing? It's an indication of honest use. I guess age will come, bringing its changes, whether I'm ready for them or not. If I expect to be anything but disappointed and unpleasantly surprised, I'd better seize the day and embrace the alterations as they arrive.

But whatever changes I embrace, I still feel fourteen years old. I wasn't very graceful then either. My feet were too big.

*Lord of eternity, may your grace*
*Hold me*
*Until I lay my burdens*
*Down.*
*Amen.*

# Somewhere Over the Rainbow

*I*t was the first picnic of the year. Family, friends, sunshine, potato salad. The kind of event where the large issue of the day is whether to sit in the sun or in the shade. There was excitement from the playoffs. I love games that go into overtime. Everything was as it should be. Heaven was probably not too far from my brother-in law's backyard.

"Two streets down on the left. Just go up the long hill. Follow the shine."

Then the clouds came in. At first they just provided new shade, movable shadow that drifted through, making the scenery more interesting. Then the sun became the exception to their rule and the wind arrived. We moved some furniture and non-weatherproof stuff. And the wind kept coming.

The clouds were now a landslide, gray tumbling masses that rolled down on us like bowling balls. There was a hint of anxiety in our comments about the weather. More wind washed in and hit the trees like waves in seaweed. We began watching the clouds.

"Look at that one." "There's a whirlpool." "It looks like a tornado." "Oh, don't say that." "Over there you can see rain." And the wind tore around the house. We hung on.

When the rain over there came over here, we went inside. The waves of wind had run past us and were now blowing someone else's lawn furniture around. Now it was just wet. There was little disappointment about the rain. We had had a day to put in the books. And we were grateful the wind hadn't taken us to Oz.

I don't like to surrender my picnics to rain. But I hope next time it rains on one of my glories, I have the wisdom to remember that backyard in heaven's neighborhood. Gratitude alters the worth of what we hold. It changes what we consider important. Who needs Oz? I've got New Jersey. There's no place like home.

Please pass the potato salad.

*Lord of heaven and earth, thank you*
*For my home.*
*May we live*
*Beneath your bow.*
*Amen.*

June

# Honeymoon

*T*he photograph is faded and a bit brown. It shows two young people standing together on a porch somewhere. They are almost painfully thin, wearing clothes cut for others. Their shoes are practical, tough. But what hits me when I look at them is the way they are smiling. It's as if there is joy within that fills their thin frames with glory. It radiates and shines from them. The way they stand there and shine it's clear they are living on love, and not much else.

When I look at them, it is hard to leave their youthful love and power back then. They look out at me and my world not as observers from some past of poverty and simple values. Their power spills out and engulfs me. They are contagious. They do not blame or judge me in my fatigue and confusion. They do not call foul at the silly complications I call important and difficult. They simply live within the power and light of their love and the infinite potential it reveals. And their life speaks so clearly it cannot be dismissed.

They clearly remind me of how close eternity is to my hand. They remind me of the touch of a June day and the magic of starlight. They remind me of iris petals and poetry. They were so rich, all because they loved. They were in Tennessee doing missionary work. It was 1932. Some honeymoon.

Years put a stamp on them, years of work and struggle and pain. Some of the lines were from laughter. And now it is the lens of memory that brings them close. But through all of that, they still shine, at least to me. Perhaps because I was made out of that love, as were my brother and sisters. But weren't we all?

*Lord of love, may the vision*
*Never fail*
*That sees beyond the years.*
*Amen.*

# Norma Jean

*I*'m getting the sailboat ready for launching. It's an experience for someone who's never had a boat before. So many doodads to discover and check and tighten and clean. Someone told me that a good chunk of sailing is messing around with the boat. All kinds of analogies come to mind, but very simply it does create a bond between boat and sailor that would not exist otherwise. I know each and every grommet, pulley, and pin. I've cleaned and scoured and sanded and varnished. I've looked at the stress marks, the worn edges, and the frayed places. In short, I've gotten to know her.

Some people consider it silly or paternalistic or downright discriminatory to assign gender to an inanimate object. I'm not sure. In my mind it is not pejorative to call my boat *she*, but perhaps that reveals my gender bias. I named it after my dog, Norma Jean. She was a wonderful companion whose presence was a joy and a pleasure to me almost all the time, but who never let me forget that she was not to be taken lightly. Norma died recently, and is missed. So, there was no variety of choices or deep consideration in the matter of a name for the boat.

Part of preparing it for the water, for venturing forth, was putting the name on the stern (that's sailor lingo for back end). I decided to use vinyl letters about three inches tall. They're rather blocky, so I customized them a bit with scissors. Norma was anything but a blocky personality. And they are red, for obvious reasons.

It was hot and sticky the June day I sat there with ruler and pencil and tape, making sure the job would reflect a spirit that walked on tiptoes and I swear could read minds. I sat there in the shade of the boat on the trailer, focused on spacing and leveling. Each bubble to be flattened, each edge to be smoothed. For that time there were no thoughts but doing the job correctly.

But when it was done and I leaned back on my elbows to consider the whole, a wave of memory came over me—more than memory. It was the experience of connection and remembrance and affection. It was the click of nails in the hall when I came home and the thud on the floor next to the chair I'd settled into. It was the cold of a nose in my dangling hand when I was reading and the look of expectation when I went to the door. It was the cower when a mess was made and the whiplash tail when I picked up her leash. All that and more came over me like a wave over the bow (that's sailor lingo for front end).

The boat dissolved as an inanimate object, and left behind was a *she*, pink nose and all. And through the mist of feeling I reached up and patted her, and said, without a thought, "Good girl."

If that's gender biased, sue me.

*Lord of life, may each day's glory*
*Move beyond*
*My eyes*
*Into my soul.*
*Amen.*

# The Deep Green of Wonder

*I* was wondering. I do that, just about every chance I get. When I wonder, it's not really about anything. It's not really a pathway that is specifically directional, like a city street with curbs and sidewalks and buildings all channeling walkers and riders one way or another. My wonders are more like the trail I saw the other day, when I was walking in the woods. It went off in a wandering direction, probably made by some critter or a few. It was as easy to step off it as to be on it. And it went, of its own accord, mostly nowhere.

I followed it, stepping over wild rosebushes and grapevines that humped over anything on the ground. Ducking under a branch I came to a brick wall, cracked and leaning, a remnant of another day when the pathways here were kept by gardeners instead of shy and wary inhabitants of the woods. It stood there, barely. It almost spoke in cracked tones of beds of peonies and young debutantes in tennis whites slowly wending their way to games whose results had more to do with flirting than with scores. Now ivy owned it and it only spoke in memories.

It was hard to leave. The trail disappeared, its makers going different ways from this spot. But it was more than inconvenience that held me there. It was as if the place was made of whispers and shades of green. Even the air was colored like the water in some protected, almost still lagoon.

Long ago sane folk avoided such places. There the presence of the faerie magic was too strong for mortal men and women. There the green seduced and held unwary wanderers until they lost time, and wondered their lives away. But that was when the world was young and reality was felt rather than measured.

Such is the country of wonder. It is the core of noticing something for itself rather than what use it might be. It is the basis of appreciation and gratitude, for until we pause and appreciate, the world remains a city street full of deadlines and price tags.

I left the broken wall, reluctantly. The path back was difficult, the trail not as visible from this direction. I came free of the woods, itching in the sudden heat, and turned back from the sun to look into the shadows. It must have been days I'd been in there. I knew then I'd return, out of the brightness of every day, into the deep greens of wonder.

*Lord of wonder, let me wander*
*Off the paths*
*Into your*
*Mystery.*
*Amen.*

# Eros

*I* extended my index finger so the baby could get a grip. She grabbed it with surprising strength and pulled it into her mouth where she gummed it, hard. I smiled at the mother. Cute kid. Then the tooth hit my knuckle.

Romantic love is a strange thing. The Greeks gave it its own word, *Eros*. I think they were right. It is different than any other experience in life. To confirm this, just look at someone who's "in love." It's hard to decide if they've got the initial stages of the new flu or have had too much caffeine. Plato said that the buds of the wings of our souls begin to grow when we are in love. And it hurts, like teething. The only thing that helps is the presence of our beloved. That's the only thing that can touch our soul so deeply.

I think it's a bit strange for me at this stage in my life to be teething. But Plato had a handle on how this crazy thing feels. It demands, it explodes, it sings, and it changes everything. It makes us human, deeply and without reservation. And it focuses all that depth on another—another human being. That's a lot of pressure on them. And just like the grind of that baby's gums, sometimes it hurts them. It hurts them because we're not all smooth and perfect. We have sharp and uncomfortable edges. The real miracle is when they don't pull back. When they stick out the pain of honest love and have the audacity to come forward and teeth on us. Then our wings grow out together and we fly, together.

I thank God for this gift of human love. But most of all, I thank God for my beloved.

Happy anniversary, Robin.

*Lord of love, may we dare*
*To love*
*In human ways*
*That we might know you*
*Better.*
*Amen.*

# July

# Chugerum

*I*'m digging a frog pond. It will have a little waterfall and water lilies and frogs. Uh-huh. A frog pond. Why is it every time I tell people about my plans they move back a step? I think it has something to do with frogs. If I said I was creating a fish pond, people might think I was eccentric, but they wouldn't get that glazed look in their eyes. It's as if we have a hierarchy of animals, some acceptable, some weird.

I had a friend who had an iguana for a pet. It wasn't as big as a dog, but it looked like it could eat cats. I never felt safe in his living room. My caveman instincts were yelling at me that I should not be relaxing with a dinosaur so close. He got along with it just fine.

I wonder if people have those same feelings about frogs? There's a swamp in the valley below the farm where my mother grew up. When we went to visit, I'd edge out at the first opportunity. Through the barn and down through the pasture into the swamp. There were granddaddy bullfrogs down there that were too proud to run away from some dumb kid. Half an hour and I'd have one. I never did anything with it. And I never took it home. But I'd look at it, down on the ground at eye level. It would look back. Its eyes were always full of the darkness of mud and black water. It was like communicating with some alien life-form. So I guess I get along with frogs.

But I'm not building a swamp. I want to see the plants and hear the water and maybe a *chugerum* once in a while. To have that kind of life in my yard makes me feel wealthy, close to the magic that runs like blood through the veins of our earth. Digging in the garden and watching the blooms break out does that as well, but water, flowing water and the life it nurtures, is more atavistic, less controlled or planned.

Pretty primitive stuff, but that kind of energy and power is in all of us. We are attracted to it like the womb from which we've come. It resonates at a deep place that no manufactured creation can. To be able to have that when I sit on my patio will be a great luxury. I may have some conversations with alien life-forms. You never know what I'll learn.

"Bud-wise-er."

*Lord of Creation, may we accept*
*Our place among*
*The bugs*
*The lizards*
*And the giraffes.*
*Amen.*

# Twinge Extermination

*I* woke up this morning ready to go sailing. It was one of those wake-ups that was not laced with groans and repeated hits of the snooze alarm. It was one of those open-your-eyes-to-a-day-that's-got-something-waiting-for-you mornings, like a treasure you have the map for. "Today marks the spot." So as I rolled out of bed and my feet hit the floor, I was feeling Norma Jean. That's my boat. I was feeling her heel over in the breeze and hearing the pings and snaps and swooshes she makes when the wind takes her off on a tack to anywhere. I was remembering where the sail bag was and considering whether I should take lunch.

Then I realized it was dark, darker than it should be for this time of year, and the noises I heard were not in my head—they were outside my window. There was wind, but instead of breeze for my sails, it was blowing a minor gale with rain.

I sat there stunned. How could this be? I had been halfway to the water before I was out of bed, and now I was carrying an anchor. I couldn't move. It was grossly unfair and wrong. The universe was not spinning or expanding or whatever it was supposed to be doing. I protested to no one in general, "Hasn't it rained enough this summer? How many days do I have left that I can get out on the water?" I don't think there is a good word to describe the combination of emotions that banged around in me as I stared out that window. Finally I lay back down. Sometimes I think better when the blood isn't draining into my feet.

Most of the time I don't feel afraid of the passage of time. I try, and many times succeed at living in and through the day, rather than worrying about losing it or failing to get something done. But once in a while I get a twinge. It's not a full-blown fear, more like a rodent named regret that's gained access to the innards of my home. At those uncomfortable times, I can hear it scratching in the walls, inside my defenses. Then I begin remembering all the moments of sun and clear breeze that wandered by without my noticing. And I hear the scrabbling of another pest named desperation chasing rodent regret there behind the wallpaper of my reasonable mind. How many more chances will I have to set Norma's sails wing to wing and run before the wind?

When I had rats—yeah, rats . . . that's a whole 'nother story—but when I had them, there was no hesitation. I didn't feel sorry for them. I called the guy who would make them go away. Call me a barbarian and an unfeeling cad, but I don't like things with little teeth running around inside my walls. They went. But who do you call when the vermin are in your own head and under your own skin?

There are no simple answers to that one. I've always had a deep suspicion that folks with simple answers to the tough questions aren't wise; they're just simple. Sometimes I wish I was less neurotic, but most of the time complexity seems more of a gift than a curse. And so shying from the obvious and simple answers leaves me with "take it as it comes and see what works." And the weird thing is that when I can do that, I'm already getting the rodents and pests driven out of my walls. It doesn't make letting go of glory less difficult, but it seems to let me get on with the process of living a lot more gracefully.

Who am I kidding? I wanted to go sailing. I moped, lip down and everything. I moped all the way down to the laundry room. I don't think there was a clean towel in the house. Doing laundry is not my simple answer to anything, except dirty laundry. God, please, may I have some sun on Friday?

*God of time and weather,*
*May I please*
*Have some sun on Friday?*
*Amen.*

# Grieving

*I*n the lines I write here, in the words and images I project on the wall of this page, there is a lot of my life for all to see. So much of what I seek to communicate is the deep sense of amazement and gratitude I experience in living every day. Most of the time it is tinged with joy. Joy that I remember even in dark times by considering the minute miracles that appear in my garden and at my doorstep.

In facing the necessity of articulating something that at least appears meaningful, I am forced to look at my experience of life and find the meaning that is there, waiting for me to stumble upon it like some treasure buried in my backyard. It is patient as it waits. It will not hurry from its resting place to blurt out its presence or its profundity. Indeed, often I hear its soft whisper only when I pause long enough to wonder and to wander through my life until I find the something about which I write. Winnie the Pooh called it a "long explore," this undirected journey that discovers so much more than that which we seek.

As I wander today, I find myself tired. And to be honest— for that is the only sort of being that works on such a journey—I am a bit afraid. It is hard to lose that which is precious, and the burden of carrying memories gets heavy. None of us are exempt from loss or fatigue. They are part of the human condition. And so is sadness.

The elves of J. R. R. Tolkien's Middle Earth are immortal. They sing and dance and appreciate the glory of life. But they are sad because they see so many things pass away. Thus my fear. I do not wish to live a life of sadness. Yet is there an alternative if we accept life with integrity, the gift as it's given, not as we'd wish it to be?

My mother was a wise one. Her strategy for facing any beast was not to use philosophy or martial arts. Theology was interesting for her, but when it came to confronting dark days or demons it was for her very secondary or twenty-secondary. She knew, like the elves, that magic is not some fairy-tale or some dark nightmare. It is part of the blood of the earth. It connects us with the source. It is the spring of wonder and inspiration. And she knew that it is accessible, available to those who would see the leaf and the feather and the bug and the child rather than merely look at them.

"So," she would say, "when are you going on your next walk through life? When are you going to see beyond the end of your nose? When are you going to let the mud squeeze between your toes and listen to that mockingbird busting his lungs from the sycamore tree? I know you're tired and sad. So dance slowly. Wander through the grass with your eyes closed and remember something you never knew. It's twilight. There is magic in the air. Look at it sparkle. Breathe it in. It belongs to you. It waits for you to discover and embrace it. It waits for you, child of life."

So you see, I found it again. Sneaky, huh? Didn't solve a thing, but on my explore I found something I didn't know I was looking for: me. I swear that woman should have had pointed ears.

*Lord of all things, seen and unseen,*
*The darkness is not dark,*
*For you.*
*Shine into mine.*
*Amen.*

# Busted

When I saw the police car's lights in my mirror, I thought the officer was in a hurry to catch a thief or help someone in distress, so I pulled over. He followed. Benjamin said, "What did you do?" And in all innocence I said, "I have no idea." But the feeling had begun. That creeping feeling that no matter how innocent you may think you are, you must have done something to deserve the attention of "THEM." I got out the papers.

The cop wanted to know if I knew how fast I was going. I had this irrational urge to get sarcastic. I wanted to say, "Somewhere below the sound barrier." I wanted to comment on the snugness of his uniform. I wanted to ask him if he slept with his gun. I wanted to ask him if he'd gone to school to learn how to be pushy. I imagine the mouse fantasizes about beating up cats. But, we're left with reality. So, in spite of my self-destructive urges, I was a good boy. I restrained myself and answered his questions truthfully. No, I wasn't paying attention to my speed, and no, I didn't know the limit was twenty-five right there.

My nephew has told me that he always talks his way out of tickets. I haven't figured out how to do that. I've tried. But I just don't know the right combination of assertiveness and friendly good ol' boy to use. It always comes out sounding slightly desperate. I feel like a limping caribou watched by a wolf who's waiting for lunch.

I think down deep I know I'm guilty. Perhaps not very guilty right now, but for all those other times when there was no snugly uniformed guy with a nightstick to catch me, I have to pay. And so I feel like I did the afternoon my father caught me smoking. I was eight or nine. Immediately, I knew. I wasn't guilty of a crime. I was a guilty person. I had to pay. The guilty always do. (He "let" me smoke a cigar about the size of Minneapolis. Sick is such a small word to describe how I felt.)

I keep hoping that the guy with the lights on top of his car will feel sorry for me and grant me amnesty. But why should he? It's his job to catch all us guilty folk and help us receive the gift of consequences.

That's one reason why I'm Christian. Forgiveness better figure big or I'm in trouble. I wonder if Saint Peter's uniform is snug? "Please pull over here by this pearly gate. License and registration, please."

> *Father forgive us, 'cause we're still stupid.*
> *May we learn*
> *And forgive us when we*
> *Don't.*
> *Amen.*

# August

# Weeding

*I* have a hard time weeding. Anybody who sees my garden knows this. Blooms climb through all kinds of lush grass and delightful vines. There are even trees here and there, volunteers brought by some natural UPS delivery system that looks suspiciously like a groundhog. I have a tendency to appreciate the weeds as much as the flowers. So instead of yanking that little cedar tree, I have to dig it up and find a place for it. Probably over there where the hemlocks are suffering from that white aphid. I love the way the sweet peas bloom, even though they tend to take over anything in the near vicinity. I don't even know what that spear-leafed guy is called, but he puts out the nicest pink flowers. And the twenty-foot monster with the dinner-plate leaves has become a pet. We call it the garden beast. Needless to say, any planning for the garden gets buried in the jungles of August.

When the frost burns down my jungle, I fertilize and dump on peat moss. And I find places to put new bulbs for blooming next spring and feeding the squirrels who are the groundhog's attendants.

Someone told me the other day that my garden was a mess. To her credit she offered to "clean it up." People try to be kind in the weirdest ways. I told her, "No thanks. I planned it that way." I offered to demonstrate how I trained everything to look so "natural." She left shaking her head and muttering. I hope I didn't blow any of her gaskets.

I think we worry too much about imposing some sort of order on nature's handy work, or on other people's partnership with living. What looks like a mess to us may be a delight to the weirdos next door.

So I was really startled when someone from the garden club asked me why I wasn't exhibiting in the annual, judged flower show. I stood there gaping as she continued, "Your iris are exceptional and those perennial sweet peas are magnificent." I wanted her to repeat what she'd just said before a notary so I could use it next time someone wanted to help me "clean up." But I can't take all the credit. I've got a partner in my effort. If I won a prize, they'd have to put the groundhog's name on it too.

*Lord of creation, if I'm a weed*
*May I be*
*Interesting.*
*Amen.*

# Sacrament

"*D*innertime!"

In our house that statement used to initiate noise similar to an avalanche. From all that sound you'd think they would have rolled into the kitchen like boulders. But they drifted in. These easy walkers could not have been the earthquakes that rattled the light bulbs. But there were no others coming to the table.

Banter was normal. Getting lined up for plates or seated for the feast was accomplished after some circling, rather like buzzards taking their time before they swoop. Finally, with a bit of pushing and shoving, they settled. Then the question, "Did you wash your hands?" Which started the whole process again with the minor addition of water fights.

It was almost a ritual. There was a comfort and a sense of security in the noise and the questions whose answers were already known.

Sacraments are that way for me. There is a cadence and an order, a rhythm that transcends the specific motions and words. It is close to dance, a movement to a score that plays in the souls of the participants. It is too meaningful to be redundant, and it is even frightening at times when the song of the spirit touches the common moments of sharing. The first time I baptized an adult, I stood there terrified. The water in my hand felt like molten lead. Surely it would burn us all. But I saw it was water, common water, a familiar gift. It is the common nature of it that helps it work so dependably. Food, drink, and water all touch us, unassuming, because we are so used to them. And then the moment owns us, and we are lifted into the dance, often in spite of ourselves.

I remember the dance of dinnertime with a nostalgic fondness that speaks to me of home in a language that cannot fade. I return to share in its poetry with great regularity. And so it is sacramental, for it lifts this moment into its embrace and creates here a sliver of that day when avalanches and water fights were part of the routine. I remember the gift as it was given with all of its common grace. And the moment shines, even though the altar boys spoke with their mouths full.

*Lord of the water and the wine,*
*Holy is your name*
*And precious*
*Are the dirty faces*
*Of your greatest gifts.*
*Amen.*

# Dog Days

*I*t's August. There are a few ways of telling. The way the sunlight and the dust get together. The way the kids lay under trees. And the way a certain question comes up in conversation: "How's your summer been?" You don't hear that question in July. Then we're sunk to our armpits in the sandy-barbecued-mosquitobite-camping-waterballoon-sailing-jelleyfish-deckreading-picnic-chlorineeyes-rollercoaster-neck-packthecar-flipflopblister-iceteasweat of summer. Somehow by August there is a sense of fatigue that makes us all look back. August is wistful.

I never quite know how to answer the question, "How's your summer been?" I'm caught between speaking of events, telling of moments of relaxation and recreation, or speaking of qualities, colors, and feelings. How do you describe a season? What do you tell?

I guess part of the problem is that I don't want to look back yet. I'm still living it. The warmth and glow of summer is still here, baking us right through the skin and into our bones. There are still clamshells to pick up and skip across the waves. There are still weeds to fight with. There are still long walks to gratefully come home from. How has it been? I'll tell you when it's over.

But part of that is just ornery. People want to know what

I've been up to and they want to tell me where they've been. I know. Maybe it's a good excuse to sit on the porch and have one of those rambling, accomplish-absolutely-nothing moments of human interaction that happen in August when all the jobs that need doing seem less important than a cool breeze. So, if you want to, I'll talk about the summer. But let's lay down some ground rules:

1. No sudden movements.

2. Cold drinks mandatory.

3. Don't be afraid to take or participate in tangents.

4. Pet the dog when it manages to get off its belly.

And most important: Don't mention September. OK?

So, "Pretty good. How's yours been?" "You want more lemon in that?" "Yeah, her nose is cold." "Will ya look at those lightning bugs?"

*Lord of Time,*
*Slow me*
*Down.*
*Amen.*

# Artifacts

*I*t comes down from the peak of the roof. It angles past the bathroom window and hangs next to the side steps. In some recent past it carried the movement and sound of Ernie Kovacs and Jackie Gleason and *My Favorite Martian.* But the intricate set of tubes and wires that netted the TV signals from the air and brought them down to be digested by our tube was replaced by a single wire, cable, and the antenna became something on the roof, unconnected and not even worth bringing down. We probably wouldn't notice it up among the trees except for the wire, garlanding down to nowhere.

There's something a bit sad about that unconnected skeleton up there. Something spooky about the wires hooked to nothing. It can probably still grab those signals. Perhaps it waits to be plugged in and wonders why no one wants what it catches.

Working within an institution always has a whiff of the artifact to it. Part of what we do as we labor within the hallowed halls is maintain that which has been important. We remember and celebrate methods and means that worked in the past. The question remains, do they still work in the present tense? We can still do all the good stuff that has been important to so many, down through the years. But why don't more people want what we net from the sky? I wonder if we with our steeples and stained glass are like that antenna, reaching and grasping the power and the glory, but the wires to people's lives are just not plugged in. Has the world passed us by?

My sense is that institutions rise shiny and cutting edge, and fall rusted and obsolete. There is nothing holy about the structures we build to house our endeavors. Indeed there is danger in confusing the two. Yet within the structures of the past are echoes of the ideals and hopes that shaped them. Ideals and hopes that can still speak to us in this later day. Pipe organs may be fossils from an era before digital synthesizers, but they sing in harmony with the power that shakes reality. So I will appreciate and remember.

There it stands atop my roof, an artifact of some when else. There is nothing to redeem it, except my own silly affection for that which served us and is now replaced by the new and improved. But perhaps that's not so silly. Affection rarely is. So I'll leave it, an icon of the days when Marshal Matt Dillon faced the bad guys and drank beer with Miss Kitty.

But the wires I'm going to cut. No sense getting tangled.

*Lord of the new, Lord of the old,*
*When I'm an artifact*
*May some weirdo*
*Find me fascinating.*
*Amen.*

# September

# Back to School

*T*his is a strange time of year. I used to hate the smell of sharpened pencils, because it meant I had to start wearing shoes again and leave the heat and freedom of summer behind. Stores get clogged with students and their support systems buying binders and rolls of brown paper for covering books. Parents stand in line at the discount department stores, loaded down with clothes and sundries. And the streets have a new obstacle to traffic flow. The yellow whales are on the road again, scooping our children into their maws and swallowing them as they swim away down the road.

Our whole world takes on a new set of rhythms. The hearts of our towns beat differently. You'd think in my exalted position of middle age, my school-seasonal angst would calm down. I mean, there are no teachers to assign me to a seat. (I hated the front of the room, though I felt more secure there.) There are no lunch ladies to tell us to keep it down when we "got going." (I still love to "get going.") There are no bullies who know all the nasty words and make me feel like the playground is a cycle of hell (though there are some people who still make me sweat). There are no ropes to climb in gym. (I envied the monkeys that went up to the ceiling without breathing hard.)

I wonder if I'll ever be able to not feel like something's dying in September. I wonder if I'll ever be able to smell sharpened pencils and not flinch.

The funny thing is that school wasn't that hard for me. I got along with the teachers and I had a lot of friends. It wasn't a horror. I loved reading books and figuring out the puzzles, "If a train leaves Cleveland at two o'clock in the morning going west and another train leaves Chicago at three o'clock in the morning going east . . ." I loved singing in the choir and the chocolate cupcakes with the white icing in the middle that I got in the school cafeteria. Mom never bought them at home. And after a while, I loved being around all those girls. But I never let them know that until I was in high school.

I drove by my high school the other day. It's a middle school now. I went around to the back and parked in the empty lot. My father took me out there one snowy day and stopped the Buick. He got out and told me to take the wheel. We skidded all over the place for almost an hour. The principal had a labeled parking place that someone—no one ever found out who—painted over in pink and relabeled "Penguin." I could see the hallway where we used to run sprints during fencing season. I could almost smell the locker room. Not one of those memories hurt. They were all part of a past that I treasure.

Somewhere in there I suffered; I remember that too. But it just doesn't seem as important as the crazy exhilaration I felt running onto the football field with the cheerleaders. I was the school mascot, the tiger. It was a great way to meet girls.

Maybe the whole thing is tangled up with letting go of that which we have and the threat of that which we don't know. Maybe we're all conservatives at heart, unwilling to take a chance on something that is full of unknowns and what-ifs. And maybe we're all just scared kids at heart, afraid to leave the warmth and security of home to venture forth into the not-so-warm and often insecure world that can judge and hurt and leave us in our pain, alone.

The funniest thing is, I'm a teacher. And when I look at those

kids—college kids get younger every year—I remember what
I felt when I left the golden days of sandy summer behind. And
I work like crazy to give them something other than a prison to
look forward to. Just like some of my teachers must have done.
And they did a pretty good job, because when I looked at that
old high school, I didn't flinch.

But I still don't like the smell of sharpened pencils.


*Lord of the edge, Lord of the expected,*
*Teach me*
*That I may grow up*
*Into eternity's surprise.*
*Amen.*

# 9-11

*T*he sky has been so blue lately. Blue enough to break your heart. But we haven't had much heart to notice. Other things have broken our hearts. Other things that are not beautiful or natural or good. They used the clear skies to attack us. The burning could be seen and smelled and tasted with every breeze. I'm glad the sky's been blue. It's less dangerous for the rescue workers, though it feels like it should be raining. It feels like all creation should be weeping.

I've been doing that lately. Weeping. It's not really crying; it's different. The tears rise in my throat and spill over at moments unexpected. Billy Joel's song "New York State of Mind" made me weep the other day. I pulled over and sat there spilling. Mayor Rudy Giuliani walking a bride down the aisle—in place of her father, who died in the attacks—did it again. It happens at times I don't expect it, and sometimes when I do there are no tears.

But few things are following the rules and systems we expect. Since that Tuesday there are questions about even the simplest things. Fears rise before us, charging "what-ifs" with deadly possibility. And victories shine in the most common events. We are unsure of ourselves. Are we able to be who we were? Are we able to go on as we used to without thinking?

In some ways, I hope not. I hope we never try to go on without thinking. The worst part of us is that which does not consider or feel or wonder, but just functions out of habit or lust or duty. It is terrifying to consider life, to realize that we are so fragile and so vulnerable that all that we have can be taken in the blink of an eye. But until we are willing to consider our fragility, we are only appetites, consuming another chunk of living.

A few have risen up and grasped the opportunity to face the terror of such honesty and moved through it in acts of unselfish glory. Some are famous, heroes we are proud to call our own. But most are just like you and me. They weep in their pain and suffer in their fear and then, laying aside all the paltry excuses and self-pity, seize the day for the incredible treasure that it is.

Times such as these call for heroes. Or perhaps, in such times heroes are more welcome because we need them to move through the wreckage to hope. Whether you feel called or just afraid, look up with me and weep. For we have been given the gift of life. And even in the midst of all this pain, the gift is still achingly beautiful. Dare to seize the day. Be a hero.

*Abide with me, fast falls the eventide,*
*The darkness deepens, Lord, with me abide.*
*When other helpers fail and comforts flee,*
*Help of the helpless, O abide with me.*
*Amen.*

# Floyd

*I* transplanted four rosebushes from my parents' house into my garden. Two of them proceeded to bloom within two weeks. Another kept shiny green leaves and demonstrated vitality graphically. The other didn't. It lost some of its leaves. It looked kind of sorry it had made the trip. Maybe it missed the salt air. Maybe it missed my mother. I've gotten into a habit of standing next to it each morning as I drink my coffee and talking to it. For some reason it seems male.

"Now come on, man, you can do this. It's a nice place. There are all kinds of new people to impress with your flowers. There are all kinds of lessons to teach with your thorns. Just give it a try. Push out a sprout or two. See how it feels."

So I'm weird. You should have figured that out by now. Over in the other bed the three stooges were busting out all over, new leaves, new stems, blooms. But this guy sat.

I was glad about them. But the slow one had become more important. It was having a rough time. So, in some strange way it created a whole new focus in my garden. It drew me as the strong plants couldn't. They were doing their own thing. This one needed some support.

So often we take the weakness of others as a liability. Actually, their vulnerability is an opportunity, not only for concern and nurture, but for listening and learning on our part. We, if we are willing, are brought to a new awareness of the need for tenderness and gentleness that strength often eclipses. It is not a sin to be weak. It is a season of life, a season that all of us experience late and soon.

The other day when I was giving my morning pep talk to my slow rose, I noticed reddish knobs at the juncture of a couple stems. I was elated. I said "Good job, man, keep up the good work." Floyd—I named him after the blunt hurricane—had put down some new roots and was pushing out some new branches. The season of waiting was over. But I had gotten into a good habit, talking to my flowers. I learned it from Floyd.

I think there's time for a bloom or two before the frost. "Go Floyd."

*God of growth and grace, may your pattern*
*Of hope*
*Be seen*
*In me.*
*Amen.*

# LBI

*L*ong Beach Island has been the family magnet since before I
came on the scene. With all the moving around we've done, it
has been a center that has held. My parents retired down there
and lived on that spit of sand and vacation homes until they left
us, one after the other. And we still go to the old house.

During the summer the place vibrates with activity and
renters. The population swells like an overblown balloon, on the
verge of exploding. One of the cops told me that once school is
out, over a hundred thousand people stomp around on the
island. You'd think it would sink.

After Labor Day a weird transformation takes place. The
water stays warm. The weather is pretty much the same, at
least for a few weeks. But the people all leave. And by October, the powers-that-be turn off the traffic lights. The same cop
told me the postseason population drops to seven thousand.

When folks hear we have a house down there, they often
tell me they appreciate the quiet of the shore after the season is over. It feels like they're expecting me to say, "Oh
yeah, me too." I nod and say "Um hmmm." I guess they
don't like crowds.

I do have all kinds of wonderful memories of the shore during the sparse times—casting with my old rod off the beach in
the October light; working in the garden in the April chill; get-

ting the fire going in the dark of February; banging pots on the front lawn on New Year's Eve—memories that come with wind and shadow and affection. There is a pride that rises from the hometown sense of being part of the island, season in and out.

We "natives" don't depend on warm weather and amusements to journey across the causeway into the teeth of the salt wind.

But in my humble opinion that goes the other way. I don't go to the island *or* abandon it just because a bunch of pale and eager tourists descend to get sunburned and party their brains out. In fact, that seasonal migration onto the beaches and miniature golf courses is just as much a part of "my" island as the coming of the clouds of snow geese to the bird sanctuary at Brigantine, just south on the bay.

When Mother and Daddy had gone, we considered selling the place—for a microsecond. Now, it's a family partnership. A bit awkward at times, but it represents too much of our roots to just pull up and out. So we've entered another season. But we still go down there and take off our shoes at the first opportunity. It reminds us of who we are. It's a constant, stoplights or no stop-lights.

Anybody want to walk down to the corner for an ice cream cone?


*God of wind and gulls, tourists and traffic,*
*May I be faithful*
*Season in,*
*Season out.*
*Amen.*

# October

# Uhhh . . .

$S$omeone told me the other day that I should take that popular herbal stimulant for the brain. I wondered at the time whether they were offering me a way to be sharper and more lucid than I already am, or trying to send me a message that I really needed some stimulating. Against my egotistical better judgment I bought some of the stuff and opened the bottle and took the brain zappers for a few days. I didn't notice any difference. I still forgot people's names and where I left my glasses and what I was supposed to do, when.

Some people have told me it's because I'm lazy or I don't care or I've got other things on my mind. Well, nobody likes to be told they're lazy or don't care. I do admit that I have a lot running around in me, probably a tad too much. But how do you say OK, everybody, my mind's on overload, I don't want to deal with any more of life right now? The kids need to be unnoticeable, the job needs to be so smooth I don't even know I'm there, and no special trips to the grocery store, please. Give me that for a couple weeks and I might remember a few names.

But it doesn't work that way. There is no way to shift into neutral. Things get tangled and there is no grace period. Now is the only time frame. So we stress ourselves into forgetfulness, probably as much in self-defense as anything. I worry about these popular management techniques that allow us to cram more into a smaller time. I wonder if we keep cramming more and more into smaller and smaller spaces, won't we reach critical mass and just blow up?

There are all kinds of ways of de-stressing, but I think the most important is making up our minds to appreciate what we've got before we run by it to the next item on the agenda, as in *consider the lilies*. It doesn't get the jobs done, but it lets the now shine.

And if it shines maybe I'll be able to call up some of the memories more clearly. But there's no guarantee to that. I think I'll still take the memory-enhancing pills. The problem is, I don't remember where I put them.

*Lord of all that is, you know us*
*All and each.*
*Forgive us when*
*We forget.*
*Amen.*

# A Mystery

*T*here are two chimneys on the west end of the roof of our house. None of the fireplaces that feed into them are active. That part of the house was built in the middle of the nineteenth century, a while ago. Back then the chimneys carried smoke and ashes up from fires that warmed parlors and bedrooms. Now no smoke comes out of them and the fires are only history, beyond anyone's memory.

But there is a mystery about these two brick pillars on our house. One of them is closed. At some point in the past a slate top was put down on it. It stands out a bit on all sides of the bricks around the chimney. It keeps out dust and squirrels and wasps. It keeps in heat that is looking for a way out. The other one has the slate, but it is held off the top of the chimney by a brick in each corner. The rain stays out, but everything else is offered a way in. Why? Why should one be sealed and one not? Did someone go up there to seal both of them and only get to one before they were interrupted? By what?

There is no way of answering those questions now. We can come up with *perhaps* and *probably*. In our quiver of conjecture there may be the answer to the mystery. But there is no way of knowing for sure. The real answer may be something we would not even imagine.

The past is like that. It is gone beyond our ability to change or to understand or even to know clearly. We are left with high points that stick out and leave evidence and indications in the present. But every day that passes obscures the whys and wherefores more completely. And we are left with assumptions that provide mysteries for our consideration today.

So here we are, between the mysteries of the unknown future and the uncertain past. And we wonder how and why and if. Sooner or later the time comes to stop wondering and to get on with the now. "Time waits for no man." I don't think it waits for women either. In this time of now we are dragged out of our wonderings about how and why and if and are given this moment to make decisions in spite of the mysteries that surround us. It is our time to take the possibility of the coming day and create a history for those to come. And in that future, they will wonder why we did what we did, and some of the theories they come up with will be insightful and close to our true motives. And some will be so out there we wouldn't recognize ourselves in our own history.

And they will judge us and what we've done with categories of value that we may not consider in this day. All we can shoot for is to leave some beauty they can appreciate and not too much wreckage for them to clean up. Perhaps that is the best hope for our labor.

But be sure that they'll look at our projects and consider us quaint primitives, for that is the arrogance of every age. And be sure that they'll consider our hairstyles and fashions funny and weird. And be sure they'll wonder why we did what we did, and why we left undone that which seems so obvious, to them.

So I still wonder why they fixed one chimney and left the other. Maybe they did it to bother some later day muser,

namely me. Either that or there was a real nice day of fishing that couldn't be missed. Or . . .?

*Lord of mystery and power, may I be*
*A blessing*
*To the ones*
*I'll never know.*
*Amen.*

# Snapshot

*I* came into my office today and found some snapshots, left by a friend on my desk. They were pictures of an August picnic. There I was floating in a pool of rippled blue. It was a good picture, relaxed and clear. But looking at it I shivered to think about being wet in the October wind that was making my office windows rattle. But wait a minute; that was August, distant from now in calendar and temperature. Then cookouts, now tailgating. The illustrated memory hadn't taken me out of the chilly now. It had only given me a window through which I saw then. But here I stood firmly planted in the deepening frost and turning leaves.

Some memories are not like that. Some are so vivid, so dominant, that their gravity drags me out of now to another time and place with all the feelings and sensations that were a part of that moment. In some cases these are peaks in my life— our wedding, the passing of my father, moving days. Some of them have an aura of glory. Some are laced with pain. These are significant moments that changed who I was and continue to be.

But there are others, seemingly small moments, yet they exert the same influence on my present tense—they pull me back to there and then. Chocolate chips scattered across the counter as my mother made cookies, my brother singing nonsense songs as he painted the roof with linseed oil and turpentine, a walk with Robin along the uneven boulders of the Sandy Hook breakwater. These are more than memories; they are so vivid they seem worlds with their own smells and textures that alter now every time I go there. The peaks are monuments in life, landmarks by which I navigate. The small moments are precious mementos of the journey.

I don't know what it is that makes the difference in my mind, what allows such moments to remain so vivid. But it makes me consider this day a bit more carefully. Because whether I like it or not, today will soon be a memory. Perhaps it will also be a place of power that draws and directs me out into whatever future I face. It would be a glory for this moment to be one of vivid joy, a monument. But it would be a blessing to claim a memento, a quiet moment on the journey from this peak to that, where forget-me-nots bloom, stirred by the passing of the mystery that is time.

Perhaps the snapshot was more powerful than I thought at first. Now it's got me wandering around in all sorts of places, warm and chilly. Besides, taking another look at it, I had a great tan.

*Lord of time, may I treasure*
*The landscape*
*Of my life*
*As you do.*
*Amen.*

# Sycamore

*A*cross the driveway is a monster. It has more dignity than any president or king who ever wielded power. It stands in all of its various moods with a stability and grace that boggles the mind. It has been right where it is for over two hundred years. It has given birth to many children. Its family lives all over town. Its name is Sycamore, and it shades my home and the backyard.

Trees are amazing creatures. They stand there, pillars for the sky. They reach up out of our world and catch the first hints of breezes, forecasting the coming weather like sailors who taste the wind and rub their bones and know without a doubt what is on the way. Their leaves on branches are roofs on rafters for shelter and playgrounds for fantasies of pirate ships and star cruisers. I know because it was to trees I went as a child to find the platforms for my flights beyond.

There were maples and elms around the house in Harrisburg where I grew up. The elms were not as willing to let me up into their branches. But they neighbored the maples that became my ladders up out of normality and into wherever I wanted to go. I would climb and consider, travel and imagine. I would hang and gain perspective, leap and learn to fly. In the trees and between them there were no barriers. The world was three-dimensional. And no matter who was looking for me, there were few who considered searching anywhere beyond the flat plain of the ground and none who ventured high enough to find me.

Sycamore is not climbable. Its first limbs begin their wandering reach from the trunk at least thirty feet above the grass. And so, most of the time it stands there, dappled pillar to the sky, another common part of the yard, ignored in the rush and passage to and fro. Yet in this time of angled light and shifting season, it rains its million leaves down into my flat world and draws my attention up and out, into its spreading communion with the sky. And I remember the rush of wind and the creak of the branches as I watched summer storms pushing across the earth, into my arms.

So when you rake those leaves, look up and see the monsters from which they've fallen, and consider their age-old dance. And if you want to be a bit of a druid, lay your hand on one of them, and consider what they have seen and felt and remembered from their deep and lofty point of view.

And if you want to climb one, be my guest. Just don't tell any other adult where you got that skinned arm. They'll look at you like you've lost your marbles. But what do you care? You've danced with the wind.

*Lord of the wind and the trees, may I look*
*Up*
*Remembering*
*How much there is.*
*Amen.*

# Disguises

*H*e wanted to be a nose!

I had scheduled a meeting with him. He was a busy seven-year-old. I had asked him simply, "What do you want to be for Halloween?" He had sat there, with his hands on his scabbed knees, and looked me straight in the eyes. "A nose." I thought I had misheard, but after I questioned, I confronted a look of quiet disdain for being so dense, and realized I had heard correctly.

His reasons for this choice of altered identity were not forthcoming. He had chosen. It was now up to Dad to figure out how to make it happen. I felt like a Rose Bowl Parade float designer. But this was more important than impressing some corporate sponsor or a panel of judges. I had to impress my son.

We do this to ourselves with great regularity. We set up our relationships with expectations hung all over them. Others expect us to be a certain way and do a certain thing and we allow that expectation to corner us. We're happy to take the credit. But what if we let them down? What if they're disappointed? What if they don't approve? Will they still appreciate us? Will they still trust us? Will they still love us? And after a while, after rising to the occasion a few times, how can we say no? Don't we care anymore?

It does feel so good to be the hero, to be seen as the creator and solver. It's hard for me not to slip into that one. When it comes down to it, I know those expectations are as much my business as anybody else's. And how can I afford to let me down? I have to live with me.

Am I neurotic or what?

But there he sat with the complete calm and confidence of a seven-year-old who still believed his dad could do anything. I heard myself saying "OK, fine." He jumped off the chair. Meeting over.

So Dad came through. A metamorphosis complete. One big nose, head to ankle. I wasn't sure what reaction he'd get from the school population. They'd probably wonder about his perverted father. But their judgment was secondary. I labored mightily into wee hours and finally received the highest commendation. "Wow!"

As the nose left the room I basked in the glory of four seconds of adoration and approval. His eleven-year-old brother stood with me. Even he'd been impressed. He turned to me at that crowning moment and said, "Dad, I want to be a foot."

*Lord who has made all things,*
*Please ignore my disguises.*
*It's only me.*
*But I guess you knew that.*
*Amen.*

# November

# We Hold These Truths

$W$hen I was eight, the vice president of the United States came to Harrisburg, where we were living at the time. I remember the strangeness of going to see such a public person, an important person, without a camera or a television in between. It was more weird than exciting. But there was an added twist that made no sense to me at the time. Everyone in the crowd was shouting, "I like Ike!" Now why would they yell that? This guy's name was Nixon. Who the heck was Ike?

I felt dumb because everybody else seemed to have no trouble with the whole thing. They seemed very excited and willing to cheer about whatever this man said, though the public address system made it sound like he was trying to talk with the mike in his mouth. *"Goo arb gla morb sentrix!"* Applause. *"Goo arb gle strig sentrix peble ib the world!"* Wild cheers. And so it went. But I got a button and my father took me out for breakfast afterward. I had eggs over easy and pork roll. All in all a good day.

I'm not sure the political dance makes any more sense to me now than it did that chilly morning in Harrisburg. Though the new digital public address systems don't mangle the words quite so badly, and the details of the process are less of a mystery to me, I listen and wonder and for all the clarity and insight I'm still left with the feeling that the enthusiasm is a lot like cheering for our team. Understanding and choice seem less important than slogans and labels.

I believe in democracy. For all its glitches and troubles, for all the general apathy and political nonattention to the critical issues, I still believe in this system of the ritual of choice. I believe in it because it is based on a dream, the dream of human dignity.

There is room for realism, room to laugh at ourselves. But cynicism that denies the power of our freedom to choose denies the truth that we are important as we are. Great or small, young or old, vanilla or chocolate, we were all created equal. So let us cheer and wave the flags, and remember the dream as we reach out and pull the levers.

To quote that great statesman, *"Goo arb gle strig sentrix peble ib the world."*

> *Lord of choice, thank you*
> *For this miracle*
> *That reaches toward*
> *Your dream*
> *Of freedom.*
> *Amen.*

# Fixing It

*T*here was a leak in my car. No vital fluids like oil or gas or brake fluid were dripping out. Water, common normal water, fell from the sky and found its way *into* my trunk. I worked on seals and latches and finally I went to the experts at the auto parts store. People work there who must have been in on the design of the Model T. They look like auto parts wizards. Ancient and wise, their thumbs are specially equipped to flip through all those phone-book-thick references and find the exact doodad to make whatever isn't right perfect. Some of the younger guys use computers. They're not as impressive.

Anyway, I came with appropriate humility to the auto parts wizard and described the problem. He didn't need to consult the tomes. This one was easy, at least for him. He came out from behind the counter and walked ahead. Obviously, I was to follow meekly. He passed the wiper blades and the antifreeze. It was across from the lubricants. A rack of glues, all kinds laid out there in their diversity just for me. He ran his finger above the various boxes and tubes and cans, down the row and then back. There, there was the one. He flipped it off the shelf and with the assurance of polished skill, slid the new tube out onto his hand. "This'll do it." It was fact. There was no question or proof needed for this truth.

Obviously, I bought it and brought it home and read the

directions and applied it. Need I even comment on the fact that it worked? Water does not invade my trunk anymore. But there is an interesting odor that comes from that direction on cold days when I run the heat and close the windows. It makes me remember the model of the battleship New Jersey I put together one summer. I had to do it on the screened porch because of the fumes from the glue. Ventilation.

This is a law of the universe. I'm sure it is as rock solid as gravity or the speed of light or how peanut butter sandwiches land when you drop them. This is another of those constants: "The cure costs. Have your nickel ready."

There are very few easy answers to any problem. And most of those answers have a bad habit of stinking in one way or another. This might cause us depression, but more appropriately, it can give us a better handle on our expectations about any situation or person, including ourselves or whatever wizards we follow, even the ones with specially equipped thumbs to consult their tomes.

But hey, now I can hang one of those Grateful Dead air fresheners on the rearview mirror. I hope the pine-fresh fumes don't dissolve the glue. And whatever you do, don't light a match.

*Lord of leaks and fixes, may I be*
*Willing to be*
*Part of the solution.*
*Amen.*

# Plumber's Flum

*I* am typing this on the same keyboard I used last week. The letters are showing up on the same screen. But, what they look like there and how they get moved around is not the same. I am using new software. There are all kinds of snazzy doodads (that's my level of computerese) in this new system that seem to make everything work more smoothly. I feel positively cutting edge.

I said "seem to make everything work more smoothly" because, if I'm honest, I'm not sure that's true. It's fun to have the new tools. It's exciting to learn to use them. But I wonder if a lot of my sense of energy here has to do with having a new toy. Sometimes I feel like that when I go into the hardware store. All those gorgeous implements of destruction, all arranged so beautifully. If I had one of those adjustable plumber's "flums," I'd be set. No more loose "doohangles" in our house. But then I keep walking and keep looking for the duct tape. Less romantic, but definitely on my list and within my budget.

I get reactionary sometimes. I get proud of being slightly out of step with what's "in." There's something of value in the arts and crafts and styles of what has been before. I touch my father's brace and his box of bits and it seems ultimately preferable to the rechargeable drill that's over my workbench. But that can get as silly as keeping up with the "new and improved" gewgaws. Snobbery, whether it is inverted or not, is still a waste of time.

Whatever my prejudices, they seem to be only part of the picture. Few of us have a grip on both now's cutting edge and tradition's dependable rock. If we try, we get slightly schizophrenic. Each of us tends to lean one way or another. It's part of what defines us as individuals. So I appreciate the computer geeks, and I expect them to drag me out of the technological quagmires burbling in my path. And I hope they have at least a passing respect for my knowledge and capability that has more to do with the uses of wolfsbane and how to jibe a sailboat. I guess we need each other; at least I hope we do. If we can hold onto that, the world will remain a lot more interesting.

Now, how the heck do I save this thing? What do you mean, "system error?"

> *Lord of all gifts, please don't let*
> *The computer eat my book.*
> *Amen.*

# Time Well Spent

*M*y appointment was for 2:15. By three o'clock everybody in the waiting room knew each other. All of us were a little uncomfortable to be there, but we all knew we needed to see the guy with the stethoscope, so we helped redefine the word *patient*. Besides, his plants were healthy and his nurses were friendly. When a spouse said he'd go for donuts, they told him where. I ordered a decaf with cream, no sugar.

I don't know about you, but waiting for someone to tell me that I'm sick, or to undress, or to pee in a cup, or that I need some attention that I don't want, makes me nervous. I begin feeling pains I never felt, I begin remembering symptoms of the black plague that resemble the cold I have. I begin wondering why I put off this doctor's appointment so long. These are not conditions conducive to allowing me to be a patient patient.

Neurotic, nervous, and slightly crazed, but patient?

But there was something in that waiting room that was different. We all giggled a bit and talked about all the things we could be doing with all the time we'd wasted leafing through magazines and admiring the molding. One guy said he'd love to be playing golf, but considering his physical condition, he couldn't do that anyway. Another patient said she was giving up time she could be billing clients for, but she wasn't sure this wasn't time better spent, at which point her cell phone rang. We all told her she was cheating. She left the room to talk.

It was a moment of strange grace. Our mutual anxiety joined and created something better, something we all needed. We shared the moment rather than stewing in our impatient juices. It is rare to find spontaneous community in our world of efficiency and cost-effectiveness, of individuality and independence. We are so insular that we miss the opportunities for the gift of human interaction that make life sweet, even in a doctor's waiting room. When did we get the idea that we don't need each other?

When the business lady reentered the room, she lent her phone to a parent to call the baby-sitter. Then the donuts came. The spouse had bought an extra dozen. He figured we'd need it. There was sugar in my coffee, but you know what? I didn't mind. And to tell you the truth, I was kind of sorry when they said it was my turn to go in to see the guy behind the door. But I told him he had the best waiting room I'd ever been in. He looked at me as if I needed a psychiatrist.

"Rev. McKirachan, do you know what day it is?"

"Yeah, Doc, it's a good day."

*Lord of love, may I claim*
*The peaceable kingdom*
*Wherever I find*
*Lions or lambs.*
*Amen.*

# Over the River and Through
the Woods

We left after supper on Thanksgiving Eve. I meant to get out earlier, but I had to pack after work and I had a hard time finding the big, hard green olives to make my part of the feast. Finally everything was stashed in the back of the Celica and the kids were belted in and we pulled out onto Route 80 headed west. It always felt like vacation when we went west on Route 80, and going to my sisters' homes for the holiday was a real break. There I was no longer pastor or administrator or even responsible father. I was part of an extended bunch who shared and supported and let me be a person. I was also the kid brother, and that has distinct advantages.

Everything went fine. "The Ocean Waves May Roll" and "Looking Through the Knothole in Grandpa's Wooden Leg" sounded great. We were in good voice and excited and happy to be going on our annual pilgrimage to the family feed. Then we passed Stroudsburg and went up into the Poconos. They're not very big mountains—more of a lumpy plateau—but the altitude creates strange weather shifts. We drove up into clouds, better known as fog. This fog was no now-and-then wispy spiderweb, spun across dips in the road. This was cement that poured and set around the car, reflecting white from the headlights and red from the taillights. The road was visible for a few feet, its presence beyond the reflected light a mystery, taken in faith.

I thought we'd run through it, so I kept on. And then I was afraid to stop. I must have passed exits without seeing them, but I could swear they'd been clogged up with this ooze that had us in its grip. I strangled the steering wheel as much to control my own fear as to control the car. Every once in a while a beast would snarl and blunder by. The truck drivers could either see better, or had lost their minds. I would follow their lights as long as I could and then slow down, alone in the milk again.

Time got very weird. The boys slept. We plowed on for at least twenty years. I began to wonder what I'd do as a retired person, when we got out of the fog. Finally the road began to dip off the plateau, out of the clouds, down to Scranton.

In the town of Clark's Summit there is an all-night donut shop, Mr. Donut. When we pulled into its parking lot, I tried to let go of the wheel. It felt like amputation. I climbed out of that car like a diver coming out of a deep-sea bell. There were glints and angles at every glance. Whole bunches of pins and needles joined the snaps and pops coming from my hands and neck and shoulders to remind me of my body. When we sat down at the counter, the kids did rotations on the stools and giggled.

I ordered two glazed and an old-fashioned with a cup of coffee. I felt like I'd missed a few birthdays up in that cloud. Between the pastry and the chocolate sundaes we were no less festive than we would be on the morrow with turkey and chestnut dressing and hubbard squash and scalloped oysters and cracked olive salad (that not being an exhaustive list). I would be most grateful for the salad, because I would be there to make it; for a few hours on that particular evening, I hadn't been so sure.

Thanksgiving is a lot more than a feast. It's an appreciation of what we have. Too often it's easy to drive right by.

We're in a hurry, after all. But once in a while we're reminded.
It's precious. It's here.

So I drank my coffee, and I ate my donuts, the glazed first.
And I thanked the waitress, and Mr. Donut and my kids and
the One who made the cloud and all.

*Lord of all that is,*
*Thank you.*
*Amen.*

# December

December

# Tilting Planet

$S$omewhere in the shifting of the season that takes us from growth and bloom to fruit and harvest, the axis of our lives shifts as well. The jammed agenda of September and October erodes the tan and re-creation that August's slow and easy days allowed. It's as if there's too much to fit into the rooms of our lives. The blue skies of Indian summer and the final invitations of warmth are eclipsed by the necessities of the calendar. And all turns brown and gray. Darkness reminds us of our fatigue as we wake to alarms and responsibilities. And we wonder, I wonder, which is life? Are we here to sail or balance budgets?

But the shift is not stopped by the gray and brown burden of October's labor. For fanged monsters, pirates, and dainty royalty claim our attention and demand sweet ransom. It is a whimsical moment that rattles the chain of dark and chill. And still the shift goes on.

November is no better—wind and freezing rain, tired cold walks home from the train in early dark. But somehow there it begins. There amid the frost and deepening night a spark of warmth is struck. It calls to even the lonely and the burdened, inviting all to remember and to share. And so it begins in feast and football and shopping. And we remember more than what has been and what we have. We remember what is to come.

And we fall in love again. And we act the fools. We are caught in sentiment and desire. Infatuated desperation drives us to do and find and give. And all our world, our dark and chilly world is lit, not with brightness but with twinkle, as if we wish to touch the night gently.

I do not understand those who shun Christmas. How can they turn from such tender glory? The world reacts as it does because it is so hungry to be embraced, though much of what we do is so clumsy. But for all our clumsiness there is a moment when the darkness and the burden of the journey become part of a dance, as if our loneliness and pain were met and used to create one clear opportunity amid all of night's dead ends. And we with two left and tired feet find the grace to waltz with the ones who sing the music of the stars.

So let the shift go on, from season to season and year to year. As long as there is Christmas there is no loss, only harmony.

> For lo, the days are hastening on, by prophet bards
>     foretold,
> When with the ever-circling years, comes round the
>     age of gold;
> When Peace shall over all the earth its ancient
>     splendor fling,
> And the whole world give back the song which now
>     the angels sing.
> Amen. *

---

* Edmund Hamilton Sears, "It Came Upon a Midnight Clear," in *The Presbyterian Hymnal* (Louisville, Ky.: Westminster/John Knox Press, 1990), no. 38.

# Some Gift

$S$he was alone as only a teenager can be, when the angel came announcing that everything she'd planned and expected was to be set aside by the choice of God. I wonder where she got the strength to accept it all. I wonder if it was so off the wall that she accepted without consideration of the cost. She understood her power. She understood how this changed things. She was no silly girl. She stood alone and questioned angels. God made a good choice.

Too often when the angels sing the songs we know—songs about her and shepherds and the cold dark night—too often we are alone and in our loneliness suffer from the distance we feel between all we've planned and expected and where we find ourselves. Our desires turn to aches as the paths to happiness lead away into other places. So Christmas is a gauntlet of regrets or sad attempts to spin the straw of now into the gold of happily ever after.

She had no assurance except her sense that this strange and wondrous stage had been set by love. She chose to accept uncertainty as the norm and reach beyond security toward stars and wide-eyed shepherds still giddy from angels' song. She considered the gifts of stable's straw and gruff strangers' awe sufficient to light her night with glory.

If only we in our crowded loneliness can remember her and

follow with our hearts toward that place of openness to the gift of now. She is not the only one who's been there. She is one of many who have been and still are willing to let the gift of Christmas overshadow all the *bahs* and *humbugs* and all the very good reasons not to become tangled in wonder. She is not alone there in the blazing light of stars and angels' song. Every one of them with her is slightly foolish for letting all this silliness seduce them from the well-worn paths of practicality. Every one of them is too vulnerable for their own good. Every one of them hopes for everything and expects nothing. Every one of them sings because their hearts have overflowed.

And every one of them knows that even in the darkness, they are not alone.

*Angels and archangels may have gathered there,*
*Cherubim and seraphim thronged the air;*
*But His mother only, in her maiden bliss,*
*Worshiped the beloved with a kiss.*
*Amen.* *

---

* Christina Rossetti, "In the Bleak Midwinter," in *The Presbyterian Hymnal* (Louisville, Ky.: Westminster/John Knox Press, 1990), no. 36.

# Commuting

*H*er brother, his son. He had gone to work and then . . . they had come because they had heard.

They were awkward, standing hunched against a chill that was deeper than any windy December day could create. They were chilled by a loss that had taken away more than one person. As the buildings had fallen, they had lost their direction, their sense of what was dependable. They came here, survivors of wreckage that was and still is too immense to comprehend.

They came to this old building, in years past a train and ferry station, where thousands and thousands of people from New Jersey had left for work, just like their boy had. But now this place was changed. It was heated and staffed and arranged to offer another kind of transition for people as they commuted from shock to grief, as they left their loved ones behind.

I was their "companion" for the day. I walked with sister and father from office to office, helped them fill out the forms. We ate together, warming soup and comforting munchies. We took the ferry together, and walked into the gray irrational landscape known as Ground Zero. We stood together as they received the flag and an urn of ashes scooped up from that place of horror and loss.

Finally we sat together in a room where symbols of all the great religions rested amid candles and silence. And we cried.

There is too much pain and loss to understand or organize or compensate. All the gestures and efforts to help the survivors and to honor the dead seem small in the face of what has happened. And the suffering goes on. The distance between grief and hope is just too great. We are caught here helpless, hunched against the cold and darkness.

We were finished, done with everything that could be done here, on this day. We walked to the big doors, three of us now awkward. He stood before me, wordless, strong from years of work and facing life, vulnerable from days of anguish and confronting death. With a rush his arms encircled me, his cheek against my chest. "Thank you. Thank you." He stepped back, again the father and provider, his arm around his daughter. "My boy is in God's hands. So are we all." And they left, out to the car that would take them home.

I stood there watching them go. Then I turned out toward the crowned lady in the harbor, painted red by the setting sun. I tried to make some sense of it all. And I remembered the words at her base: "Send me your tired, your poor, your huddled masses yearning to breathe free . . . . I lift my lamp beside the golden door." It came to me that she has been celebrating the journey of the awkward and the lost for a long time. And these two had come here in that tradition. They had commuted from their private pain to the embrace of a concerned nation. Their journey was not done, but perhaps now begun. I realized that they had given me a gift. They had let me share the beginning of their journey.

This gift we are offered in this season—sharing the journey. It comes to us where we are. It offers us God's companionship. Christmas is not for winners. It is for the ones who need miracles just to get by. It is for those of us who feel the weight of sorrow's pain and grief's burden. It is for those of us who journey in the night not knowing where to go, but hear that somewhere there is an open door and a warm place, and perhaps a caring companion to hold our hand and bless us on our way.

> *And ye, beneath life's crushing load, whose forms*
>   *are bending low,*
> *Who toil along the climbing way with painful steps*
>   *and slow,*
> *Look now for glad and golden hours come swiftly*
>   *on the wing;*
> *O rest beside the weary road, and hear the*
>   *angels sing.*
> *Amen.* *

* Edmund Hamilton Sears, "It Came Upon a Midnight Clear," in *The Presbyterian Hymnal* (Louisville, Ky.: Westminster/John Knox Press, 1990), no. 38.

# The People Who Walk in Darkness

*T*he alarm goes off in the darkness. I climb out of bed and stumble over shoes I didn't put away last night, discovering a table leg with my toes. I'm not used to turning on a light when I wake up in the morning. It doesn't seem right. Morning should be bright, or at least have the intimations of brightness. This blackness is of the night, not the morning. It's intimidating to have such a basic altered. It makes me feel small and powerless. Especially when I stub my toes.

When I was in fourth grade, I learned there were people in the world who didn't care if I lived or died. Chief among them was the ogre of the playground. He didn't look very ogrish. He looked like a brash fifth-grader who let the world know with great regularity that he was the toughest item around. He had a crew cut and an incredible ability to make me feel like a mess to be cleaned up. Recess was his kingdom. He held court, with ridicule his scepter. It was not fair. Recess was to be a time of liberation, moments of freedom from structure and authority. The ogre was a new form of authority, whose only goal was to humiliate and limit me.

In the morning darkness, nursing my stubbed toes, it seems the universe is run by an authority related to the ogre I feared then. It seems to humiliate me in my powerlessness and leave me to curse it in the darkness. I must defend myself with lamps and therapists to navigate my own home and my own personality. It's not fair.

But sitting there in the winter's dark, I can see, out a window, some whimsical soul has left their tiny lights on, through the night, or made it past the shoes and table legs to grace the predawn with those splinters of celebration. They illumine nothing. They do not push or shove or humiliate or contest with the night. They are a song, quiet though insistent in their shine. They grace the darkness and turn it, gentle palm to cheek, a caress to say, "Look through the darkness, there is more."

Though an intimidated child, I knew it then. Though sometimes bruised and confused, I know it now. It is no ogre that tilts the world and turns it toward a new day and year. It is the One who gave a child to light the dark, and Christmas to remember that gentle love still shines, even through our night.

So celebrate, but watch your toes.

*How silently, how silently, the wondrous gift is given!*
*So God imparts to human hearts the blessings of*
    *His heaven.*
*No ear may hear His coming, but in this world of sin,*
*Where meek souls will receive Him, still the dear*
    *Christ enters in.*
*Amen.* *

---

\* Phillip Brooks, "O Little Town of Bethlehem," in *The Presbyterian Hymnal* (Louisville, Ky.: Westminster/John Knox Press, 1990), no. 43.

# Journey to the Manger

*H*e was three and a half. His brother was eight. And we were preparing for a pilgrimage into the heart of Christmas. New York City is not an easy place to visit at the best of times, but in these final weeks of December? The world comes and goes and gawks and spends and adds to the perpetual storm system of human endeavor that is the Big Apple. People told me I was nuts to attempt such a trip, let alone to bring my children along. I agreed but thought it would be good for them. Ah, the silly arrogance of parents.

My friend Bill Monroe was going along. He was an older man who'd never been married or had children. He didn't own a car and spent a lot of time at the New York Library researching genealogies. Why he wanted to go with us into the maelstrom was a mystery.

We went on the bus and in no time the windows were marked with noses and chubby fingers. Questions were quieted with a running account of where we were and "Look at the bridge." "Look at the airplane." "Look at the oil refinery." And finally, "Look, there's New York." That skyline never ceases to amaze me. How could anyone imagine that? The kids thought so too, for about thirty seconds. By the time we pulled into the cavern of Port Authority, I was frazzled and pooped.

We disembarked into the flow. I've always wanted to go down the Colorado River on a raft. Those rapids are nothing compared to making your way through the Christmas crowds, clutching your children. Ben, the younger, was on my shoulders. Bill and I took turns grasping various parts of Jon's anatomy. We got them soft pretzels. When I combed the crumbs and salt out of my hair later, I thought of the mysterious knee-high mustard stains some people must have wondered about when they arrived wherever they were going.

I began to remember what all the sensible people had said, about how nuts it was to come here, right where I was. I began to regret all this and wish, as so many have and still do, that we could do this with less craziness and more peace. But we must make the best of this, so let's stick to the agenda. Forward ho!

The Met was crowded. What a surprise! What wasn't? We got in and wandered through the maze of masterpieces and wondrous curios. Somewhere past the armor, the medieval room vaults up and makes room for the angel tree. It is a miracle of Neapolitan craft and artistry. These beings full of the power that any messenger of God must wear like a skin cascade down the huge tree like some migration that has found its way home. Below them spreads the crèche of hundreds of figures, most of them going about their business, some of them traveling to see the current spectacle. And in its midst, amid the ruins of Imperial Rome, is a family with a new child, a baby.

Jon had stopped pulling away to see and touch. He stood still, his hand resting in mine. Ben's weight rested quiet on my shoulders, his arms encircled my head. And then amid the hush of the room he said with the volume of a child overwhelmed, "Ohhhh! It's Christmas."

The day changed for me, right there, right then. The whole messy, threatening, chaotic jumble was transformed. I understood with my heart again and found the gift, wrapped up just for me. And whether they were just going about their business and this whole thing was a bother or whether they were there to gawk or whether they really knew the depth of the gift that it's all about, everybody was part of it, part of the pageant, part of the gift.

My little ones are grown and Bill has left this life behind, but I can still feel a small hand in mine and arms encircling my head. And I still hear the words of wisdom and wonder that are for all of us no matter our condition of life, "Ohhh. It's Christmas."

God bless us, everyone.

> *O holy Child of Bethlehem, descend to us, we pray;*
> *Cast out our sin and enter in, be born in us today.*
> *We hear the Christmas angels their great glad*
> *    tidings tell;*
> *O come to us, abide with us, our Lord Emmanuel!*
> *Amen.* *

---

\* Phillip Brooks, "O Little Town of Bethlehem," in *The Presbyterian Hymnal* (Louisville, Ky.: Westminster/John Knox Press, 1990), no. 43.